820.9   Mulder, John R.
Mulde     The temple of the mind: education and
        literary taste in seventeenth century
        England.  New York, Pegasus, 1969.
            165 p.   (Pegasus backgrounds in English
        literature)

RELATED
BOOKS IN     1. Gt. Brit. - Intellectual life.
CATALOG      2. Gt. Brit. - Religion.  I. Title.
UNDER

                                            72135

# The Temple of the Mind

*Education and Literary Taste in*

PEGASUS NEW YORK

# The Temple
## of the Mind:

*Seventeenth-Century England* ℣

*111206*

John R. Mulder

This book is one of a series, Pegasus Backgrounds in English Literature, under the general editorship of John R. Mulder, New York University.

# Acknowledgments

The author and publisher are grateful to the following for permission to reprint material contained in this volume:

Doubleday & Company, Inc.
  *The Complete Poetry of John Donne,* ed. John T. Shawcross (1967),
  *The Complete Poetry of Robert Herrick,* ed. J. Max Patrick (1963),
  *The Complete Poetry of John Milton,* ed. John T. Shawcross (1963),
  *The Complete Poetry of Henry Vaughan,* ed. French Fogle (1965)

Cambridge University Press
  Sir Thomas Browne, *Religio Medici,* ed. J.-J. Denonain (1953)

The Clarendon Press
  George Herbert, *Works,* ed. F. E. Hutchinson

Random House, Inc.
  Andrew Marvell, *Complete Poetry,* ed. George de F. Lord (1968)

*For my parents*

# Preface

The variety and virtuosity of the seventeenth century make it difficult to reconstruct a background in which every writer might have his niche. On the other hand, the library of specialized books and articles dealing with nearly every aspect of the age has grown too large for assimilation by the student, who is often at a loss to know how to make use of so much erudition in his reading of Donne, Marvell, or Milton. The purpose of this book is to bring some of the magic of scholarship down from the mountain and into view for the acolyte.

The focus is emphatically literary: to quicken the student's response to individual works rather than to increase his theoretical knowledge of seventeenth-century trends and problems. Many topics of legitimate interest have therefore been excluded: the influence of one writer on another, the importing of ideas from abroad, and the vexing question of the definition of those critical terms 'wit,' 'metaphysical,' and 'baroque.' Instead, this study deals with significant aspects of seventeenth-century education. I am not advancing the thesis that the education accounts for the literature, or, in other words, that the second is a product of the first. A knowledge of the curriculum of the period does, however, help us to recover the way in which Browne or Herbert was read by his contemporaries; and such knowledge is likely to bring us closer to the author's intention.

Seventeenth-century education differed from the modern variety in the importance it accorded to eloquence and religion. I have therefore devoted three chapters to each of these areas. School-masters and college tutors trained their students in language, logic, and rhetoric (Chapter one). This emphasis nurtured a particular kind of literary taste: a fondness for logical, often dialectal structure (Chapter two) and a delight in word play (Chapter three).

Although the period was one of religious controversy, its devotional literature is "beyond the strife of confutation" (Chapter four). A convenient synopsis of the religious ideas that writers took for granted in their audience is the standard catechism used in the grammar schools (Chapter five). The received method of biblical interpretation included the theory of types, a knowledge of which is necessary for our understanding of the function of biblical allusions and images in the poetry and prose of the age (Chapter six).

The literary examples that I have analyzed in order to illustrate the theories are mainly taken from the metaphysicals and Milton, for the very reason that these writers challenge the modern reader most. My analyses are not offered as complete explications but as suggestions about certain details of style. I have tried to indicate approaches that the student might want to continue on his own.

For their part in the remoter preparation of this book I am grateful to professors Austin Warren and Frank L. Huntley, both of whom taught me to read and interpret. I wish to thank Marymina Wallis, who gave invaluable aid in the research for the first three chapters. Professor J. Max Patrick, my colleague at New York University, and Professor Joan Webber of Ohio State University thoughtfully commented on my work and saved me from many errors, doubtful generalizations, and over-readings. I owe a special debt of gratitude to Professor Daniel L. Eneman of Rutgers University for his advice, encouragement, and patient help in revising various drafts of the manuscript.

Southampton, N.Y.
September, 1968

# Contents

*The Temple of the Mind*

# Chapter One

# The Educated Reader

## Some facts and uncertain figures

We cannot compute how many Englishmen read Donne's *The Songs and Sonnets* or Milton's *Paradise Lost* in the seventeenth century. It is easier to say who did not read them; we know that the London printers marketed their books to all classes save the hewers of wood and drawers of water whose hands were their only portion. After 1500 the curious English version of the democratic ideal put the merchant within reach of a title, but it kept the servant out of his master's library. Even the democratically inclined Levellers, who defended the rights of the people in the 1640's, included under *the people* all males except servants.[1] This means that one half of the nation looked upon the other half as merely a vast number of hired hands. Nowell's *Catechism,* after asking why even servants should keep the Sabbath holy, gives this alloy of refined and gross arguments:

> . . . surely meet it was that servants should, together with us, sometimes serve him that is the common master of them and us; yea, and father too, since he hath, by Christ, adopted them to himself as well as us. It is also profitable for the masters themselves that servants should sometimes rest between their workings, that, after respiting their work awhile, they may return more fresh and lusty to it again.[2]

This condescending attitude is poetically preserved in Herrick's "The Hock-Cart," where the laborers are reminded that the harvest festival is only a moment of respite:

> . . . this pleasure is like raine,
> Not sent ye for to drowne your paine,
> But for to make it spring againe.[3]

Although England gave little thought to the education of the working class, its schools under the early Stuarts were remarkably democratic in comparison with those of continental Europe. They were accessible to the sons of landowners, lawyers, doctors, merchants, artisans, and tradesmen. Moreover, they were located in every corner of the realm. At the time of the Restoration, the country provided one school for every 4,400 of the population. Seven generations later, when a wearied Matthew Arnold inspected the educational system, there was one school for every 23,750 souls.[4]

Almost all of the schools available in 1660 had been built during the previous 120 years, and many of them were endowed with private money. The donors were often men of Puritan leanings, who believed that they would have to account to God for their husbanding of the wealth entrusted to their stewardship. They held, of course, that they could not thus procure their salvation; but they also believed that good works are, if not the cause, then certainly the effect of the grace of God. In other words, not everyone who does good is saved, but every man who is saved does good. The distinction proved to be beneficial for the public welfare of England; one might be damned before God but appear saved, at least in the eyes of the world, through one's munificence. Therefore the rich merchant or landowner often tried to settle his account with God before leaving this world, establishing trusts and funding endowments as 'secondary' evidence of his salvation. Other motives, equally intelligible but more profane, included the desire to leave a name, to maintain a record of achievement, or to compete with another benefactor of conspicuous generosity.[5]

Their zeal for religious reform made many donors wary of giving to the established Church. Before the Reformation, it had received more than half of the gifts donated for charitable purposes. Under Elizabeth, the Church's share waned to ten per cent. It rose again under James I and Charles I to almost eighteen per cent, but much of that was wrung from the laity to pay for the repair of the many church buildings that were nearly ruined through neglect.[6] The merchants and the gentry preferred to leave their money in places where it could be effectively controlled by other middle-class people of like persuasion, or at least not drained off for sinecures. They left funds for the building of almshouses and hospitals, for prison reform, and for the beautification of their native towns; set up trusts that would furnish loans to anyone starting a business or trade; and even provided dowries so that an impoverished gentlewoman need not face the anguishing choice of either starving to death or marrying beneath her station. Education received the largest share of the available money. Under the early Stuarts, private funding of education was especially generous. The middle-class donors not only endowed grammar schools, but also founded new colleges at the universities and enlarged the endowment of existing ones; they established scholarships in grammar schools and in the universities. When Charles I ascended his throne, almost ten per cent of the approximately 5,400 students enrolled at Oxford and Cambridge were poor boys on scholarships; in 1640, more than half of the men who sat down for their Long Parliament were university graduates.[7]

The promoters of education under the Tudors and early Stuarts were sure that Christian and humane learning would cure nearly all social ills; it would root out ignorance and, consequently, poverty; it would establish the light of God in what they regarded as the darkness spread by Rome; it would open the door of advancement to young men and thus contribute to the peace and progress of the realm. Yet when Hobbes inquired into the causes of the Civil War, he found the universities guilty of breeding sedition. This peevish criticism is still the easy argument of porcupine conservatives and was as suspect then as it is now. The universities were in the business of educating minds; unfortunately, they produced more intelligent minds than were gainfully employed in service to the Church or to the State.[8] Robert Burton's "Digression on the Misery of Scholars" enumerates the problems of those young men who were carefully educated only to be callously neglected. From his chamber in Christ-Church Burton followed their careers attentively, for the outlines of his picture have not required revision by modern historians. He complains of the greatest scandal of the time, the swelling corruption of the establishment: "this evil has invaded the middle and highest classes, men of eminence, not to say bishops . . . . For

ofttimes the very highest men are perverted by avarice." One either
swam with the current or drowned; converts to the venal system
were preferred, "whilst in the meantime we that are university
men, like so many hide-bound calves in a pasture, tarry out our
time, wither away as a flower ungathered in a garden and are
never used." Burton expresses too the acute sense of frustration
that attends the waste of unused talents, "the least of which,
translated to a dark room or to some country benefice where it
might shine apart, would give a fair light and be seen over all."
Many a graduate who spent all of his patrimony in those long
years of study that require "a body of brass" must take to "teaching a school, turn lecturer or curate, and for that he shall have
a falconer's wages, ten pounds per annum and his diet or some
small stipend so long as he can please his patron or the parish."
Merit alone rarely got one preferment: A man might be of "good
parts, good words and good wishes," but a rich patron "will not
prefer him, though it be in his power, because he is *indotatus,* he
hath no money." The scholar could enter into his promised land
only through the "simoniacal gate." Many a university man in
holy orders had to hire himself out as the private chaplain of a
noble family for little more than the cost of his food and clothing.
Burton calls the type a "trencher chaplain," whose living was
always precarious: "if he offend his good patron or displease his
lady mistress in the meantime . . . he shall be dragged forth of
doors by the heels, away with him!" [9]

One allows, of course, for a certain amount of gusto and exag-
geration in Burton's rendering. He himself confesses that he
intends no disparagement "to the very many in the Church of
England, exceptionally learned, eminent, and of spotless fame,
who are more perhaps than any other nation in Europe could
produce." He also admits that there are among the patricians
"many well-deserving patrons and true patriots of my knowledge,"
although his sequel may have been intended ironically: "besides
many which I never saw, no doubt, or heard of."

The discontented intellectuals made up only fifteen to twenty
per cent of the university men.[10] Yet in a time of economic and
political unrest this proved to be a dangerously large number. The
good wits that were ill-employed by king, courtier, or bishop were
available to the opposition and did much to give it prestige and

persuasive power. Burton forebodes in an almost prophetic passage: "The eagle in Aesop, seeing a piece of flesh now ready to be sacrificed, swept it away with her claws and carried it to her nest; but there was a burning coal stuck to it by chance, which unawares consumed her young ones, nest and all together. Let our simoniacal church-chopping patrons and sacrilegious harpies look for no better success."

The reading public did not consist of university graduates only. Oxford and Cambridge together awarded approximately 450 degrees each year, but London alone counted thirty endowed schools, a large proportion of them being grammar schools.[11] The majority of pupils left their desks to become apprentices in the crafts and trades. An apprentice lived seven years with a master in order to qualify for the 'freedom' of a company or guild. The apprentice apothecary studied the medicinal properties of plants and their combination into potions; the barber surgeon had to acquire a knowledge of anatomy; to qualify for a trade, one studied accounting and commercial law. Among the poets of the age, Herrick was once apprenticed to a goldsmith and Ben Jonson to a bricklayer.[12]

The grammar schools, the companies, and the universities nurtured an audience with a taste for literary echoes and allusions and a love of learned symbolism and allegory. Modern state occasions call for the concrete display of national power in weaponry and endless lines of marching troops; but when James I, accompanied by his entire household, made his first royal procession through London, he stopped at each of eight triumphal arches to sample some Latin oratory and to admire the messages of the decorations. One arch represented the Garden of Plenty as the abode of the Nine Muses and the Seven Liberal Arts; another depicted the Fountain of Virtue with its guardians Fame, Euphrosyne, and Circumspection.[13] These fancies served not only for the delectation of the court; they were also admired by the artisans, tradesmen, and apprentices among the onlookers. We tend to find more than a touch of pedantry in these allegorical displays, in the rarefied symbolism of Jonson's masques, in the pompous tone of the elegies in numerous memorial volumes. Pedantry being the by-product of hard academic labor, it is not surprising that the public pose of the seventeenth century is often bookish: Learning was then a matter of strenuous discipline and exacting work.

## The schoolmaster's method

The demands made on the young student are carefully set out by Charles Hoole in his *New Discovery of the Old Art of Teaching Schoole,* published in 1660 although probably written earlier.[14] The Reverend Hoole, a graduate of the Free School in Wakefield and of Lincoln College, Oxford, apparently found no preferment in the Church and spent the remainder of his life "in this despicable, but comfortable employment of teaching school," first at the Free School in Rotherham and afterwards at several private schools in London. His credentials are therefore impeccable. He insists that his method is based both on his own practice in the classroom and on his knowledge of that of others. The *New Discovery,* which sets out how to scale the heights of learning from petty school through lower grammar to upper, is a true schoolmaster's effort; the Reverend Hoole abhors idleness and unruliness in children. Yet his book is also the most complete source of our knowledge of the authors studied in each form and the method used in their interpretation.

Hoole, after Erasmus and Cicero, held that it is as natural for a child to learn as it is for a beast to go, a bird to fly, or a fish to swim. The city child was packed off to petty school at the age of four or five; in the country, owing to the distance from school, he would enter at the age of six or seven.[15] The country boy often started out early in the morning because the hours at petty school were from eight to eleven and one to four during the winter months; in the summer the master made use of the longer daylight hours by keeping him till five. His little mind was kept busy for four years:

> The whole Petty Schoole may not unfitly be divided into four formes; whereof the first and lowest should be those that learn to know their letters, whose lessons may be in the *Primar.* The second of those that learn to spell, whose lessons may be in the Single-Psalter. The third of these that learn to read, whose lessons may be in the Bible. The fourth of those that are exercised in reading, writing and casting accounts, whose lessons may be in such profitable English-Books as the Parents can best provide, and the Master think fittest to be taught.

At the age of eight or nine, when the child could read English with some proficiency, he was ready to enter a grammar school. The curriculum was remarkably uniform throughout England. Certain textbooks were prescribed by royal decree, but the fact that nearly all the schoolmasters had been trained at Oxford or Cambridge was probably more effective in producing uniformity. Some schools were, of course, better than others. Generally speaking, those in the cities and larger towns were superior because they employed not only a master but also one or more assistants, or 'ushers' under his direction. The schools invariably taught Latin; nearly all of them also taught Greek because a knowledge of the latter was expected of boys who wished to matriculate at the universities. Only the very best schools introduced the older pupils to Hebrew. The finest instruction was to be had in London, "which of all places I know in *England* is the best for the full improvement of children in their education, because of the variety of object which daily present themselves to them, or may easily be seen once a year."

The master of the grammar school seldom bothered with the drudgery of teaching writing and arithmetic. In the countryside, penmanship was taught by traveling penmen, who stayed at each school for a month to six weeks out of the year. They were much in demand at the end of April and in early May: The academic year usually began at Easter, and the schoolmaster appreciated receiving the first exercises of his new scholars in a legible hand. The London boys used their leisure hours at noon and in the early evening to attend a writing school. Having mastered the art of penmanship, they went, again in their leisure hours, to accounting schools for the study of arithmetic or 'merchants' accounts.' It often happened that children of quality, whose parents never contemplated their going into trade, knew no more of arithmetic than the addition of simple sums, a feat they might remember from their days in petty school. Samuel Pepys, M.A. of Cambridge, did not learn the multiplication tables until his position as clerk of the acts of the Royal Navy made it mandatory; he was then thirty years old.[16]

Modern psychologists of education may find that vacations were then not long enough to relax the children. They stayed at home for ten days or so at Christmas, Easter, and Whitsuntide. There was no such luxury as an extended summer vacation. The summer months, in fact, were meant to encourage study, the trip to school being easier, and the classrooms undoubtedly more hospitable because less damp and cold than in the winter. Happily, the routine of daily attendance was often interrupted because there were at least twenty-five holy days during the year on which the entire population, servants included, officially rested. In addition, the students could petition the master for a playday in those weeks that offered no holiday; this meant that they spent the afternoon in supervised games on the school playground.

If vacations were brief, school days were long:

> Though in many Schooles I observe six a clock in the morning to be the hour for children to be fast at their Book, yet in most, seven is the constant time, both in Winter and Summer, against which houre, it is fit every Scholar should be ready at the Schoole. And all they that come before seven should be permitted to play about the Schoole, till the clock strike, on condition they can say their parts at the Masters coming in; else, they are not to play at all, but to settle to their books as soon as they come.

There was a recess from eleven to one, and the scholars were dismissed at five o'clock on Monday, Wednesday, and Friday; at four on Tuesday; and on Thursday at three. After they had spent Saturday morning in rehearsing the grammar lessons of the entire week, the afternoon was free. In a few schools, Westminster for one, there was a brief recess at nine in the morning, but the Reverend Hoole objected to such laxness in those institutions that opened at seven rather than six A.M. At some grammar schools, the course of study ran through eight forms; at others, it was divided into six. Hoole found that the latter was the more desirable practice.

Most of the teaching hours were devoted to the acquisition of linguistic skills. Ben Jonson spoke for every schoolmaster when he declared that "Language most shewes a man: speake that I may see thee. It springs out of the most retired, and inmost parts of us, and is the Image of the Parent of it, the mind. No glasse renders a man's forme, or likenesse, so true as his speech." [17] Our image of our ancestor is the not so flattering picture of the caveman, but the forefather of seventeenth-century man was a noble Adam, as wise and gifted as Milton rendered him. Man was made in the image of God, his mind dimly reflecting the divine mind, his word retaining a vestige of the power of God's creating Word. *"Speech,"* said Jonson, "is the only benefit man hath to express his excellencie of mind above other creatures." In all the countries touched by the Renaissance, the humanists had extolled eloquence; consequently the seventeenth-century schoolmaster devoted his time to teaching every variety of speech for all possible occasions, intimate or public, ornate or plain, witty or serious.

The reason for the stress on eloquence derived from the proposed end of education, which was to fit a man for a life of service to his country. Scholarship was not its own reward. Such early humanists as Erasmus, More, and Colet were public figures. In his dedication of the *De copia verborum et rerum* (1513) Erasmus enthusiastically praised Colet "for the rare, and truly Christian piety of your spirit, because in all the efforts and all the studies of your life you never consult your private advantage but always consider how to be of best use to the country and your countrymen." [18] Four generations later, Milton defined education as "that which fits a man to perform justly, skilfully, and magnanimously all the offices both private and publike of peace and war." [19] This conception is basically a version of the old Roman ideal, meant for children who would some day take command of one area or another of civic responsibility. Although the continued increase in the number of students produced more qualified men than could be employed in the service of the realm, the rationale for the course of study was not thoroughly re-examined. The attitudes of the early humanists toward ancient history, classical languages, and the pursuit of eloquence remained the foundation of the curriculum.

The first onus on the child entering grammar school was to learn that "profitable language," Latin. This tongue grew of course more profitable by and by; the system itself perpetuated it:

> For first there are few children, but . . . may be so far grounded in the Latine, as to find that little smattering they have of it to be of singular use to them, both for the understanding of the English authors (which abound now a days with borrowed words) and the holding discourse with a sort of men that delight to flant it in Latine.

The usefulness of Latin that Hoole urges should be evident to the non-Latinist who is anxious to get the gist of Burton's arguments in the *Anatomy of Melancholy,* a work that often resembles a bilingual performance.

The basic text of the lower grammar school (the first three years) was *Lilies Grammar,* the famous introduction to Latin by William Lily (1468–1522), first headmaster of St. Paul's School. A succession of royal decrees prescribed his text for all schools in the realm. It was one of three books with which every educated Englishman was intimately acquainted, the others being the Bible and the Book of Common Prayer. At the end of three years the study of grammar had incorporated *syntaxis, figura,* and *prosodia.* This means that a child of eleven or twelve knew how to construe a simple, compound, and complex Latin sentence; that he recognized the figures of grammar and managed to vary his sentences artfully by changing the diction or the order of words; and that he was able to scan Latin verse in various meters. He would also have read, in Latin of course, such edifying works as the New Testament and the Book of Proverbs, the *Eclogues* (1503) of Baptista Spagnuoli (also known as Mantuan), selections from Sebastien Châteillon's *Six Books of Sacred Dialogues for the Improvement of the Language and Morals of Children* (1552), and the *Colloquies* of Vives and Erasmus from a popular collection put together by Christopher Helvicus (1581–1617).[20]

Upper grammar school began in the fourth form with the study of rhetoric: Schoolboys learned to identify the numerous rhetorical figures (figures of words, figures of sentence, and figures of thought) and to distinguish figures from tropes.[21] If, as was usual, the school offered instruction in Greek, it was first practiced on the fourth-form scholar. In the continuing study of Latin the composition of elegant letters was now begun. The most important matter to be read, however, was the comedies of Terence, whom the students had to make "wholly their own," not for fun, but for grave aesthetic, moral, and practical purposes, because

> Terence, of all the School-Authours that we read, doth deservedly challenge the first place, not only because *Tully* [Cicero] himself hath seemed to derive his eloquence from him, and many noble Romans are reported to have assisted him in making his Comedies, but also because that Book *is the very quintessence of familiar Latine, and very apt to express the most of our Anglicismes withall.* The matter of it is full of morality, and the several Actors therein,

most lively seem to personate the behaviour and properties of sundry of the like sort of people, even in this age of ours.

In the fourth form the boys also tasted the delights of the Muses through a serious inquiry into the art of Ovid's *Metamorphoses*. The method of analysis was as follows: Each scholar had to memorize half a dozen verses, then construe the passage verbatim, parse it grammatically, list all the tropes and figures he could find, give the derivations of words, and show the extent of his Latin vocabulary by finding synonyms for them; after that he must scan each verse. So far, the pupil had performed only half of the usual assignment. Next, he must turn Ovid's passage into elegant English prose in order to turn it back into proper Latin, "rightly placed according to the rules of rhetorical composition"; finally, he had to unscramble it again into a variety of English verse.

The Reverend Hoole recommended the introduction to comparative grammar (Latin and Greek) for the fifth form, which was also the year taken up by oratory. The pupils read the speeches in Sallust, Livy, and Tacitus, and the orations of Demosthenes, Isocrates, and Cicero. For further profit in poetry there was Virgil, "the Prince and purest of all Latine Poets." Hoole found that, after he read the *Eclogues* and the *Georgics* with his students, "they can be left on their own for the *Aenead*."

With his introduction to oratory, the art of persuasive eloquence, the schoolboy began to compile his own commonplace book, looking for any kind of matter that might help him in an argument: brief and pointedly moral histories out of Plutarch, Livy, Pliny, and others, fables and adages, hieroglyphics, emblems and symbols, ancient laws and customs, and so forth. Such a medley was usually subdivided into sections: one being a collection of witty sayings, another a record of rhetorical ornaments, a third a list of descriptions of things "natural and artificial." The intellectuals of the age kept and added to this compilation during their lifetimes. The best-known surviving example is that of Milton, whose commonplace book is brief and collects mainly arguments and illustrations on those topics that interested him, such as virtues and vices, divorce and freedom, law and monarchy. More typical is Bacon's miscellany, which he called the *Promus of Formularies and Elegancies;* it is specifically rhetorical in aim. Bacon gathered in it every kind of verbal trick that might show his quick wit to best advantage: witticisms, proverbs, pointed phrases, analogies, set formulae for beginning and ending a speech as well as for making transitions from one part to another, retorts in debate, and re-partee. A great many books were at hand to help the schoolboy to master such elegancies. Since Erasmus' collection of maxims in *Adagia* and of similies in *Parabolae,* educators had compiled their versions of phrasebooks. Each school library was supposed to have its share of these *Phrases, Compendia, Thesauri,* or *Silvae.*

The committed faith in the virtue of verbal manipulation led Erasmus to fill half a dozen folio pages in *De Copia* with variations on this thank-you-for-your-letter note: *Tuae litterae me magnopere delectaverunt.* The Reverend Hoole found that the line *Est mea spes Christus solus qui de cruce pendet* ("My hope is only in Christ hanging from the cross") can be transposed in 104 different ways. This feat is paltry, however, compared to the verbal athletics of John Stockwood in his *Progymnasma scholasticum* (1597), who discovered 450 variations for one Latin distich.

Besides the phrasebooks, the other convenient items in the school library were the dictionaries. The early Renaissance dictionaries of Latin and Greek were partly encyclopedic; they included proper names and places followed by a summary of known facts about them. The best-known of these was the *Dictionarium* of Ambrosius Calepine (1502), which was first a Latin and later a polyglot dictionary. In his *Thesaurus Linguae Romanae Britannicae* (1565) Thomas Cooper dealt separately with the names of historical, legendary, and mythical people and places. This *Thesaurus* was the standard encyclopedia in English schools till the early seventeenth century. (Hoole still recommended it.) Cooper's popularity was transferred to the *Dictionarium* of Charles Stephanus, first published in 1593 but continually re-edited with expanded entries thereafter. In translation the title of Stephanus' dictionary reads: *An historical and poetical dictionary, containing all the ancient and modern words for races, men, places, rivers, and mountains that are needed for the understanding of the sacred and profane histories and the legends of the poets.*[22] The dictionaries were a source of profit not only to the schoolboy in search of matter for composition: They were also mined for allusions and ornaments by poets long out of school, such as Jonson and Milton. The latter acknowledged the usefulness of the dictionaries by intermittently working on the compilation of a *Thesaurus* of his own.[23]

For the scholars in the sixth form, Hoole recommends the study of Hebrew, "which is very necessary for all such as would be acquainted with the Original of the Bible, and is not very difficult to attain to, because it goeth word for word with our English, and is not so copious in words as the Greek and Latine." This advice was rarely taken; Hebrew was usually deferred until the university, and it was casually treated even there.[24] It is often thought that Milton's *Tractate on Education* must have been intended for prodigious children because he recommends in passing that to the study of Hebrew "it would be no impossibility to adde the *Chaldey*, and the *Syrian* dialect." This aside probably seemed less egregious to his contemporaries, for Hoole advises that the pupils "explicate the words of the Bible according to their several languages: *viz. Hebrew, Chaldie, Samaritane, Syriack, Arabick, Persian, Aethiopik, Armenian*, and *Coptick*, which is a kind of Aegyptian tongue."

Virgil, "the Prince of Poets," had been studied in the fifth form. Now—in their final year—the boys read "the Father of Poetry," Homer, as well as Pindar, Euripides, Sophocles, and Aristophanes in Greek. They perfected their Latin with Horace, Lucan, Martial, Persius, and Seneca, in addition to which the "merry Comedies of Plautus . . . may be easily read over." Their oratorical prowess was exercised through the imitation of Pliny's *Panegyrics* and the speeches of Cicero and Quintilian. Finally, they practiced their poetic talents by composing, in English, Latin, and Greek, a variety of verse forms: anagrams, epigrams, acrostics, epithalamia, epitaphs, and eclogues.

This course of study may seem astonishing to us, but the Reverend Hoole insists that it is "contrived *according to what* is commonly *practised* in England and foreign countries; *and* is in sundry particulars *proportioned to the ordinary capacities of children* under fifteen years of age." He sums up his trust in the usefulness of the system, declaring that

> in six (or at the most seven) yeares time (which children commonly squander away, if they be not continued at the School after they can read English and write well), they may easily attain to such knowledge in the Latin, Greek, and Hebrew Tongues as is requisite

to furnish them for future studies in the universities, or to enable them for any ingenious profession or employment, which their friends shall think fit to put them upon, in other places.

## The tutor's guidance

The control exercised over the adolescent at the university was as strict as that of his grammar school days, but it was much more dignified. Except for variations in detail, both Oxford and Cambridge enhanced the gravity of learning by the observance of formality and ritual. The emphasis on ceremony is clearly evident in the Laudian Code for Oxford, tentatively applied in 1634 but confirmed as the *Codex authenticus* two years later.[25] The code was typical of its conservative author, William Laud, archbishop of Canterbury and chancellor of the university. It aimed at uniformity of practice among all colleges; it created no new procedures, but merely regulated ancient practice. Every freshman signed in at a college or hall. Within two weeks, he accompanied his tutor to the vice-chancellor for the ceremony of matriculation, or admission to the faculty of arts. If sixteen years of age or older, he swore to obey the university statutes, took the Oath of Supremacy, and subscribed to the Thirty-Nine Articles of the Church of England. If not yet sixteen, he subscribed to the articles only.

Once admitted, the scholar attended two kinds of lectures: the *lectiones domesticae* (those given within his college) and the *lectiones ordinariae* (public lectures established by royal decree and delivered to the students of all colleges in the university buildings known as the schools). After two years the student became a sophist by successfully disputing three questions in logic (*disputationes pro forma*) before four moderators. At the end of this disputation one of the moderators delivered a brief eulogy of Aristotle; then the candidate received a copy of Aristotle's logic and the first mark of distinction, the sophist's hood. As a sophist he debated at least once every term with younger scholars still disputing *pro forma*. He also responded twice to his superiors, the bachelors of arts, in the Lenten disputations. Thus, after twelve terms, or four years from matriculation, he might initiate the ritual that would eventually give him a degree. For this, he first asked permission from the head of his own college. Permission granted, the master of his college had to "supplicate" on the candidate's behalf at four successive sittings of the congregation (our faculty senate) while the candidate stood, bare-headed, outside the door. After the final *supplicat,* the proctors of the congregation walked down either side of the aisle as the members whispered *placet* or *non placet.* If none were opposed, "grace," or permission to take the degree, was given. On the very day of receiving grace, the candidate made his *circuitus,* going around the colleges to be examined by four regent masters. He then requested the university proctors to summon the congregation at which he might be admitted to the degree. One of the proctors arranged a *depositio,* which meant that nine bachelors were asked to bear witness to the candidate's integrity. Finally, the sophist was taken by the hand, by the master of his college, and presented to the vice-chancellor, who permitted him "to lecture on any book of the logic of Aristotle." Once admitted, the new bachelor still had "determine," that is, participate once more in the Lenten disputations.

The requirements for the degree of master were equally formal. The bachelor debated thrice on questions proposed by a master. He took part at least once a year in disputations in the schools and gave six lectures of his own contriving. In his third year he sued for his degree in the same manner as the bachelor, via *supplicat, gratia, circuitus,* and *depositio.* Upon admission, the last demand made on him was called "inception," which meant his taking part in one more set of public disputations.

The curriculum at Oxford and Cambridge incorporated the ancient distinction between arts and sciences. According to Sir Francis Bacon "there are two ends of tradition of knowledge, the one to teach and instruct for use and practice [the arts], the other to impart or intimate for re-examination and progression [the sciences]." [26] The modern word for art, as the seventeenth century understood it, is *methodology.* The undergraduate practiced first of all the arts of logic and rhetoric, or the rules of clear thinking and correct expression. The arts were therefore means to an end. Having mastered the logical and rhetorical precepts, one was supposed to apply them in the investigation and dissemination of the sciences, which dealt with things as they are. Undergraduates were introduced to the sciences of ethics, metaphysics, physics, mathematics, and cosmography. Of these, mathematics was summarily treated, and cosmography, in consequence, scarcely touched upon.

In obedience to the university statues, the scholars had to attend the public lectures in logic, rhetoric, ethics, physics, and metaphysics, but the rule was more honored in the breach than the observance. After 1600 the authorities frequently complained of the diminishing attendance in the schools.[28] There were at least three reasons for this, none reflecting a lack of diligence on the part of the students. First, the lecture in the schools was the only method of teaching in the Middle Ages, when the professor possessed the only copy of the text. But in the England of the early Stuarts, textbooks were available to every student. Second, the royal decrees—some of them dating back to Henry VIII—that had instituted the public lectures also prescribed the matter to be taught. The English reverence for precedent, especially royal precedent, kept the content of the lectures almost unspotted by the notoriety of new-found knowledge. An inquisitive student soon discovered that the lecturer in the schools delivered established but antiquated views. Finally, in the Middle Ages the purpose of the universities was to train young men for the priesthood. In the early years of Elizabeth's reign, this was still the end of academic instruction because her father's break with Rome had caused a shortage of clerics who could be trusted with the care of souls in the Church of England. In the latter half of the sixteenth century, the composition and outlook of the student body began to change: The worldly sons of gentlemen of quality went up to Oxford or Cambridge in increasing numbers, if not in the pursuit of knowledge, then to acquire at least a veneer of it. The instruction in the schools, therefore, often no longer corresponded to the students' needs.[29]

In the 1570's, the upper classes might have been content to get their sophistication secondhand from books with such alluring titles as J. Sturmius' *A Ritch Storehouse or Treasure for Nobilitye and Gentlemen which in Latine is called Nobilitas literata*, translated into English by T. Browne (1570). But at the turn of the century, young gentlemen and noblemen seem to have made up one half of the university population.[30] Noblemen enjoyed the advantage of obtaining a degree in one year less than the commoners, on the apparent assumption that their blue blood guaranteed intellectual acumen. Some of the aristocrats received degrees without any effort whatsoever: On the occasion of the king's visit to Oxford in 1605, forty-three members of the royal train were made masters. The poet Richard Lovelace, of a prominent Kentish family, received his master's degree on another such occasion in 1636, two years after his matriculation at Oxford. Such degrees were not honorary—the *gradus honoris causa* was an eighteenth-century innovation—but, as Anthony à Wood calls them, "degrees of creation." The greatness thus thrust upon one conferred the same privileges as the degree that was laboriously acquired. Sons of noblemen whose academic status was not instantly advanced by royal command seldom took a degree. They often arrived with their own tutors and a staff of servants and, partially following the prescribed course of study, read merely in those subjects that were likely to furnish them with the requisite polish for advancement at court.[31]

The gentry, more practical, often sent their sons to the Inns of Court to make them adept at the sort of legal quibbling with which they could later defend and increase their patrimony. Sir Walter Raleigh was briefly at Oxford and at The Middle Temple, a course followed later by John Aubrey; Donne went from Oxford to Cambridge, and from there to Davies Inn and Lincoln's; Henry Vaughan also divided his education between Oxford and London.

To sum up, the ready availability of textbooks, the antiquarian content of the public lectures, and the changes in the make-up of the student body gradually transferred the burden of instruction from the university schools to the individual colleges; and as the public lecture declined in importance, the tutorial system came to replace it. The stringent criticism by Bacon and Milton of the scholasticism of the universities ought to be understood as directed primarily against the method and content of the public lectures. Oxford and Cambridge were still capable of stimulating young minds, but it was from the tutor that the student obtained his real education.

At first glance, the instruction provided by individual tutors might be expected to produce students of widely varying outlook. In practice, however, the tutor did not adapt himself to any student's personal interest; in modern parlance, his instruction was not child-centered. He filled his pupil in on the new knowledge that was left out of the lectures in the schools. Moreover, the accepted aims of education, the stress on classical letters, and agreement on standard authors made for a fair degree of uniformity. Even if different tutors assigned different texts, the method of reading and explication remained the same for all.

The freshman began with the study of logic, copying a brief outline of the art as his tutor dictated it to him. Next, he progressed through logic texts of increasing difficulty, till he was ready to read those works that dealt with controversies in logic. He learned ethics, physics, and metaphysics in the same way, moving from the tutor's synopsis through the standard textbooks to issues of controversy. The scholastic handbooks were of similar format, alternating a pronouncement of Aristotle on a particular topic with learned commentary on every detail of the philosopher's wording. In preparation for the scholar's real test, his disputation as senior sophister, he was encouraged to grasp at every opportunity for debate. In his first four terms he argued with his tutor and with the fellow students of his college; promoted to sophister, he became an official participant in the disputations both in his own college and in the schools.

Aside from his study in the major undergraduate subjects (logic, rhetoric, ethics, physics, and metaphysics), the student worked his way through a program of largely classical reading drawn up by his tutor. The Reverend Richard Holdsworth, D.D., fellow of St. John's College from 1613 to 1637, and master of Emmanuel for six years thereafter, recorded a reading program for scholars under his tutelage.[32] It includes, for Latin, selections from Cicero, Quintilian, Terence, Ovid, Virgil, Horace, Sallust Petronius, Martial, Juvenal, Persius, Seneca, Lucan, and Statius. For Greek, Holdsworth recommends Hesiod, Homer, Theognis, Pindar, Theocritus, Plutarch, and a number of tragedies and orations. In addition, the undergraduate was to study such varied manuals of style as Valla's *De elegantiis linguae latinae* (1471), Caussin's *De eloquentia sacra et humana* (1630), and Vossius' *Rhetorices contractae* (1621). It is evident that the list of classical authors prescribed by Dr. Holdsworth does not differ greatly from the one recommended in Charles Hoole's *New Discovery*. The difference lay in the depth and breadth of the knowledge to be acquired by the university student. He read more widely in what are now called 'background studies' on classical mythology, history, and geography in order to be able to discourse more learnedly on his favorite ancient authors. Basically the undergraduate did on his own what he had earlier done under the hourly supervision of the master of his grammar school. Again he kept a commonplace book in which he took note of the elegant verbal inventions of others, and he made up many a rhetorical composition as practice for one requirement for his degree, the delivery of a public declamation.

Such was, very briefly indeed, the schedule of studies. If the matter crammed into one day—private reading, tutorial sessions, lectures in the colleges and in the schools—now seems excessive, it may help to know that the undergraduate woke early to his tasks: Cambridge lectures began at seven in the morning, and those at Oxford as early as six, after obligatory attendance at prayers in the college chapel.

## The indivisible trinity: logic, rhetoric, and ethics

The compass of Renaissance thought embraced many divergent and newly popular philosophies, but the wisdom of Plato, Epicurus, Epictetus, Sextus Empiricus, or the mythical Hermes Trismegistus never replaced the authority of Aristotle in the educational system of the period. Aristotle was for Jonson "the first accurate *Criticke*, and truest Judge; nay the greatest *Philosopher*, the world ever had; for, hee noted the vices of all knowledges, in all creatures, and out of many mens perfections in a Science, hee formed still one Art." For the educator, one of Aristotle's most commendable features was his alleged comprehensiveness, although this trait was usually the result of the neat rearrangement of his writings by other hands. Comprehensiveness and rigid arrangement are features, if not of Aristotle, then certainly of Aristotelianism. Those who are not struck by the thought of Thomas Aquinas' *Summa* often marvel at the pursuit of detail through the seemingly endless branching off of propositions. The seventeenth-century counterpart of the *Summa* is Burton's *Anatomy of Melancholy*, serially divided into Parts, Sections, Members, and Subsections. Renaissance educators were proud of what they called their *systems*, manuals for every discipline, in which Aristotle's thoughts on that topic had been 'improved' by reordering them into a more methodical sequence.[33]

Of the main undergraduate disciplines, logic and rhetoric were the most eagerly pursued. The traditional approach again went back, through Quintilian and Cicero, to Aristotle. This approach, established by ancient authority, created no sharp distinction between the two arts. It consisted of five steps: The eloquent man had to *invent* arguments, use his *judgment* to dispose them in the best order, find a graceful *elocution,* exercise his *memory* to be able to recall his speech, and *deliver* it with the appropriate voice and gesture. The first step, invention, involved the study of *topics* or *places,* that is, the discovery of whatever points may be made on the subject. Aristotle, both in his logic and rhetoric, had advised that one examine a subject from a variety of angles, but Cicero's *Topica* was the best-known guide to the invention of arguments.[34] It lists seventeen *places,* or approaches that will furnish an intelligent rhetorician with matter for discourse on any subject: One can open with a definition of the subject, then divide it into parts, play on its name, or compare it with words of the same root; this may be followed by some remarks on the characteristics of the subject's genus and species; one can further argue about its causes and effects, its antecedents and consequences; for greater amplitude there are still available a number of topics that tell the audience what one's subject is inherent in, similar to, different from, opposed to, or incompatible with; and for lack of other evidence one can always find support in the testimony of others.

Having invented the arguments that fit the subject and the occasion, the student went on to exercise his judgment in their arrangement into an appropriate order, or 'method.' He might proceed from the particular to the general, or vice versa; he could introduce the subject as a question and debate it pro and con; a speaker sometimes chose to expand his matter into a continuous discourse (Burton's *Anatomy*) or delivered his convictions in a series of aphorisms (Browne's *Christian Morals*).

Although the manuals tried to distinguish logical 'topics' and 'methods' from rhetorical ones, it is evident that *invention* and *judgment* were used by philosopher and orator alike. Peter Ramus, a sixteenth-century professor at the *Collège de France,* saw no need for his students to study invention and judgment twice, once from the logic system and again from a manual in rhetoric. He insisted therefore that rhetoric was only a matter of elocution and delivery, and that invention and judgment were solely the provinces of the logician. Ramus and his disciple Omar Talon, or Talaeus, gained quick popularity. After the 1580's numerous Ramist manuals of logic and rhetoric were published in England. Milton himself wrote *A Fuller Institution of the Art of Logic, arranged after the method of Peter Ramus.*

During the past twenty years scholars have come to look upon Ramus as the initiator of important cultural changes. He is said to have divorced thought from speech by conceiving of thought as an independent process that afterwards can be turned into words. Ramist influence is thought to have advanced logic at the expense of rhetoric and, in consequence, to have nurtured the taste for 'wit,' 'conceits,' and 'strong lines' in the metaphysical and baroque poets. Even the eventual dismissal of traditional elo-quence by the Royal Society has been laid to a distrust of rhetoric on the part of Ramus and his followers.[35]

These views on Ramus are still debated. One reason for Ramus' popularity was the brief, methodical, and pedantic arrangement of matter in his texts, which made him eminently teachable. But it is still difficult to discern the influence of Ramist rhetoric in the style of *Paradise Lost,* Milton's professed admiration for Ramus notwithstanding. It seems that Milton found the Frenchman pedagogically useful; he claims in the preface to *A Fuller Institution* that, unlike other logicians, Ramus does not confuse logic with physics, ethics, and theology. Milton's interest in educational method, therefore, may account for his producing a version of the Ramist manual. The cultural significance of Ramus is a matter for the historian of ideas, who with the gift of hindsight may judge a phenomenon in terms of its later, sometimes very much later, effects. There is insufficient and contradictory evidence that the seventeenth-century reader was aware of the possible shattering effect of the innovations of the late professor of eloquence and history from Paris. No matter under what heading, 'invention' and 'judgment' were still taught; the authority of Ramus did not replace that of Aristotle, and for most readers thought remained wedded to the word.

Ben Jonson, always somewhat conservative because of his dependence on the court and noble patronage, expresses the prevailing orthodoxy:

> The conceits of the mind are Pictures of things, and the tongue is the interpreter of those Pictures. The order of Gods creatures in themselves, is not only admirable, and glorious, but eloquent; Then he who could apprehend the consequence of things in their truth, and utter his apprehensions as truly, were the best Writer, or Speaker. Therefore *Cicero* said much, when hee said, *Dicere recte nemo potest, nisi qui prudenter intelligit* [No one can speak skilfully without sound understanding]. The shame of speaking unskilfully were small, if the tongue only thereby were disgrac'd; . . . disordered speech is not so much injury to the lips that give it forth, as to the disproportion, and incoherence of things in themselves, so negligently expressed.

This passage confidently expresses the belief that language is the image of truth. Jonson shared this belief with his contemporaries, who were convinced that man in the innocence of Eden had possessed a fullness of understanding that conveyed to him immediately the proper word for every created thing. The Bible identified language with reality: "And out of the ground the Lord God formed every beast of the field, and every fowl of the air; and brought them unto Adam to see what he would call them: and whatsoever Adam called every living creature, that was the name thereof" (Gen. 2:19). In *Paradise Lost* Adam expresses his view of the correspondence between words and things as he tells Raphael of that incident:

> I nam'd them, as they pass'd, and understood
> Thir Nature, with such knowledge God endu'd
> My sudden apprehension . . . .
>
> VIII, 352–54[36]

Although the Fall had darkened human understanding, man strove to find the language that could render reality exactly; what God had granted Adam in "sudden apprehension," the scholar hoped to acquire through the diligent labor of logic and rhetoric.

From the belief in words as capsules of truth sprang a distrust of the fiction of poets. Plato had denigrated poetry for misleading reason by the portrayal of images twice removed from real Ideas, and for debasing the soul through an appeal to the emotions. Sidney may have written *The Apologie for Poesie* to answer Stephen

Gosson's puritanical attack on poets as liars and deceivers. A generation later, Ben Jonson mediates ingeniously between the opposing parties: The poet's art is "an Art of imitation, or faining; expressing the life of man in fit measure, numbers, and harmony, according to *Aristotle*. From the word ποιεῖν, which signifies to make or fayne. Hence, he is call'd a *Poet,* not hee which writeth in measure only; but that fayneth and formeth a fable, and writes things like the Truth." In other words, poetry is *truthful fiction.* In the *Advancement of Learning* Bacon damns the poet with faint praise: "Poesy is a part of learning in measure of words for the most part restrained, but in all other points extremely licensed, and doth truly refer to the Imagination, which, being not tied to the laws of matter, may at pleasure join that which nature hath disjoined, and so make unlawful matches and divorces of things." [37] Throughout the discourse that follows, Bacon's impatience with poetry is barely disguised, for "it hath had access and estimation in rude times and barbarous regions, where other learning stood excluded." Allegories, parables, and fables were in ancient days invented for the easier instruction of the vulgar sort of people, "because men in those times wanted both variety of examples and subtilty of conceit." As he leaves the subject of poetry, Sir Francis' transitional sentence sums up his attitude: "Let us now pass on to the judicial palace of the mind, which we are to approach and view with more reverence and attention." [38]

In theory, Bacon and his contemporaries did not conceive of art as an independent area of human experience with its own norms and its own end. Oscar Wilde would have been even less comprehensible to them than he was to the jurymen at his trial when he opined that a beautiful object is neither virtuous nor wicked, but simply beautiful. Wilde's view implies that a work of art arrests the attention of the audience and produces a moment of exhilarating but "disinterested" contemplation; the listener or viewer is disinterested in the sense that he loses himself in his surrender to the aesthetic experience provoked by a work of beauty. Such an experience is unmixed: One cannot simultaneously enjoy aesthetic delight and be prey to moral revulsion. However, Bacon's survey of the areas of human knowledge did not include the study of aesthetics. In his age, art was far more a means to an end than an end in itself. Poetry, being a means of expression, was part of rhetoric, and it was either good or bad, depending upon the moral purpose of the poet.

Seventeenth-century educators insisted on the kinship between logic, rhetoric, and ethics. Logic, which furnished the rules of lucid thinking, was first of all the road to the discovery of incontrovertible truths. When, among divergent positions, no undeniable evidence was available, logic could establish probable truths. But the logician could also use his syllogisms to defeat an opponent, no matter which side the truth might be on. Rhetoric, as the art of persuasion, was directly related to logic. This relationship was often illustrated by Cicero's comparison of logic and rhetoric to the closed fist and the open palm respectively. Committing himself to a logical proposition, the speaker had to convince his audience of its truth, or its likelihood, or its desirability over the stand of his opponent. Milton calls the combination of the two disciplines "those organic arts which inable men to discourse and write perspicuously, elegantly, and according to the fitted stile of lofty, mean, or lowly," and he urges exercise in logic "until it be time to open her contracted palm into a gracefull and ornate Rhetorick." [39] Ethics completed the trinity of requirements for eloquence because of the temptation inherent in the use of rhetoric; if logic appeals to reason, rhetoric sways the emotions, and may be used to persuade men of falsehood and to provoke them to dishonorable or unethical conduct.

The most ignoble of rhetoricians and a pattern of all wicked orators to come is Milton's Satan. As a public speaker Satan is a virtuoso: His rhetoric sways his legions in heaven and hell, deceives Eve into reaching for the forbidden fruit, and still attracts the readers of *Paradise Lost* to his party. The contrast between Satan's impassioned oratory in Books I and II and the Father's logical discourse in Book III does not, however, imply an unqualified rejection of rhetoric on Milton's part. The seventeenth-century schoolboy might discover as many rhetorical figures in the speeches of the Deity as in those of Satan. To say that God is a logician and the Devil a practitioner of rhetoric is to exaggerate the contrast. The difference in their eloquence is one of motive. The Father's rhetoric is less emotional because his argument is a chain of incontrovertible truths delivered to a receptive audience. Satan's appetite for power turns him into a rhetorician who must defend his position by all available means in front of a disheartened band of followers. His understanding is not so darkened that he does not know the truth about himself. In his soliloquy, early in Book IV, he admits that not God but he himself ordained his hell; his torment is eternal because he cannot adopt an inferior posture:

> But say I could repent and could obtain
> By Act of Grace my former state; how soon
> Would highth recall high thoughts, how soon unsay
> What feign'd submission swore: ease would recant
> Vows made in pain, as violent and void.
> For never can true reconcilement grow
> Where wounds of deadly hate have peirc'd so deep:
> Which would but lead me to a worse relapse,
> And heavier fall: so should I purchase dear
> Short intermission bought with double smart.
> This knows my punisher; therefore as farr
> From granting hee, as I from begging peace . . . .
>
> IV, 93–104

Satan cannot admit this truth in front of his infernal army or seated on his throne in the council chamber of Pandemonium. On these occasions he hides his logical sleight-of-hand behind an impressive array of rhetorical colors. (The fallacies in his reasoning have caused some critics to denigrate him as a fool. On the contrary, Satan is aware of the import of his oratory, and he is all the more Satanic for knowing that his arguments are false.) He is an excellent rhetorician, but a wicked one. Milton saw no danger in "a gracefull and ornate Rhetorick"—*Paradise Lost* is a monument of that art—but he was well aware of its possible perversion by an unscrupulous practitioner.

The frequent abuse of rhetoric had long been recognized. Bacon complains that "the government of reason is assailed and disordered three ways, either by the illaqueation of sophisms, which pertain to Logic, or by the juggleries of words, which pertain to Rhetoric, or by the violence of the Passions, which pertains to Ethics." [40] He finds that rhetoric mediates between the two other disciplines: "the duty and office of Rhetoric, if it be deeply looked into, is no other than to apply and recommend the dictates of reason to imagination, in order to excite the appetite and will." Appetite and will must be urged to desire the good, and hence "it is the business of rhetoric to make pictures of virtue and goodness, so that they may be seen."[41]

The poet being, according to Jonson's definition, the "nearest borderer upon the Orator," poetry was a subdivision of rhetoric. Its purpose was the improvement of conduct, and the excuse for its "fiction" was its potential for moral edification. Milton calls poetry "less subtle and fine, but more simple, sensuous and passionate" than prose. Sidney had defended the poet because the latter raises man's aspirations to the level of the ideal ("nature's world is brazen, the poet only delivers a golden"). Bacon expands that concept as follows:

> Therefore, because the acts or events of true history have not that magnitude which satisfieth the mind of man, poesy feigneth acts and events greater and more heroical; because true history propoundeth the successes and issues of actions not so agreeable to the merits of virtue and vice, therefore poesy feigns them more just in retribution, and more according to revealed providence .... So as it appeareth that poesy serveth and confereth to magnanimity, morality, and to delectation.[42]

Bacon's view is an oft-repeated commonplace. For Milton, poetry's value is moral and therapeutic, and poetic talents are "the inspired guift of God rarely bestow'd, but yet to some (though most abuse) in every Nation: and are of power beside the office of a pulpit, to inbreed and cherish in a great people the seeds of vertu, and publick civility, to allay the perturbations of the mind, and set the affections in right tune . . . ." The poet is the ideal teacher of virtue "to those especially of soft and delicious temper who will not so much look upon truth herselfe, unlesse they see her elegantly drest . . . ."[43] Herbert's admonition at the beginning of *The Temple* is a more succinct version of the same idea:

> Hearken unto a Verser, who may chance
> Ryme thee to good, and make a bait of pleasure.
> A verse may finde him, who a sermon flies,
> And turn delight into a sacrifice.
> "The Church-porch," 3–6[44]

In his somewhat shrill preface to the second edition of *Silex Scintillans*, Vaughan declares that "a *good* wit in a *bad* subject, is (as *Solomon* said of the *fair* and *foolish woman*) *Like a jewel of gold in a swines snowt.*" And Ben Jonson, in a less religious but still ethical vein, delivers the affirmation: "the Study of [poesy] (if wee will trust *Aristotle*) offers to mankinde a certaine rule, and Patterne of living well, and happily; disposing us to all Civill offices of Society."[45]

One effect of the utilitarian view of poetry is the strict division between style and content. Milton, for example, looked for a subject that he could "pensil [paint] . . . over with all the curious touches of art."[46] One contemporary critical cliché was *ut pictura poesis;* poems were verbal paintings, and the rhetorical figures were accordingly called *colors.* In Western Europe, painting was, at least until modern times, an obviously representational art, and in the seventeenth century a poem also had to have a recognizable referent.

A second consequence of the desire for edifying poetry was the demand for moral and intellectual greatness in the poet. Personalities with such different life styles as Jonson and Milton believed that the way to accomplishment in writing included rigorous attention to self-improvement in order to acquire ethical insight and wisdom. According to Milton, "he who would not be frustrate of his hope to write well hereafter in laudable things, ought him selfe to bee a true Poem, that is, a composition, and patterne of the best and honourablest things."[47] When Vaughan defines Herbert's imitators as producers of "those wide, those weak, and lean *conceptions,*" it is because "they aimd more at *verse,* then [spiritual] perfection."[48]

As the end of rhetoric, including poetry, was ethical, the end in most cases also justified the means. Provided he was morally upright in motive and purpose, the speaker or writer might use every argument to advance his case. The usual division of arguments into three kinds of proofs was as ancient as the texts of Aristotle: logical proof to convince the reason, ethical proof to engage the moral sense, and pathetic proof to sway the emotions. If the first kind analyzed the speaker's proposition, he often used the second kind to illustrate his integrity of character. An awareness of this function of ethical proofs helps us to evaluate correctly the touch of selfishness and egocentricity sometimes found in the literature of the period. Some critics object to the occasional vanity of Sir Thomas Browne in the *Religio Medici* and especially to the supposed arrogance of Milton. In the case of the latter, it has been alleged that his self-portrait in his *Second Defense of the English People* is dishonest. For instance, Milton does not mention his rustication from Cambridge, nor does he note that he supped with the English Jesuits in Rome; on the other hand, he writes that the merchants of Naples rumored that these same Jesuits were laying a plot against him on account of his outspoken defense of the Reformation.[49] The contemporaries of Milton and Browne interpreted these autobiographies as testimonials in which the writer attempted to gain the approval of the audience by showing that he had always been on the side of virtue, justice, and right religion. Milton's self-portrait is a deliberate use of ethical proof. To mention his rustication or his supper with the Jesuits would have gone counter to Milton's rhetorical intention; his *Second Defense* is, after all, a defense of the Protestant English nation against attack from abroad, and he has to present himself as a true son of the Reformation. If a contemptuous reference to the hospitable Jesuits can advance his case, no scrupulous observance of the amenities prevents him from including it. We should notice, however, that he makes no outright accusation: He merely says that *rumors* of a plot circulated in Naples. As for Browne's attempt to portray himself as an aristocrat of the spirit, coupled with his dismissal of other views as belonging to "vulgar heads," he used this as ethical proof to dissociate himself from "the generall scandall of my [medical] profession."[50]

Pathetic proofs, arguments that move the audience to laughter or pity, delight or anger, admiration or hatred, offered the speaker a great deal of scope. They were especially useful in the ceaseless pamphlet warfare of the age. The sarcasm, invective, and scurrility of those debates often shock the modern reader. Milton's handling of such mean devices is masterful, and many of his admirers find this unworthy of him. Yet Milton's scurrility in his pamphlets is neither more nor less than was expected in that genre, and was as zealously practiced by his opponents. An audience trained in logic and rhetoric was meant to delight in the skillful handling of the various kinds of proof. An author who introduced a sophism was fully aware of the falsehood, but he also knew that a truly outrageous falsehood would amuse his readers. Acting on that assumption, Milton has the gall in *Of Prelatical Episcopacy* to damn an unknown bishop for bearing the same name as a well-known person of dubious reputation.[51] The vehement language of abhorrence, the threats and curses of many a pamphlet, should more often be considered as tricks of style than as serious expression of the author's conviction. Many of the postures adopted by the seventeenth-century writers were understood to be affectations. To accuse such men of unscrupulousness in their use of logic and rhetoric is beside the point. There is in their technique no element of 'hidden persuasion.' They addressed themselves to people who read well, who knew a true syllogism from a false one, and who could tell figures of speech from literal truth. Through their education, author and reader shared a set of logical and rhetorical conventions, and verbal games were played according to those rules.

# Chapter Two

# Disputatiousness

### "Loves Progress"

Who ever loves, if he do not propose
The right true end of love, he's one that goes
To sea for nothing but to make him sick:
Love is a beare-whelp born; if we o're lick
Our love, and force it new strange shapes to take,          5
We erre, and of a lump a monster make.
Were not a Calf a monster that were grown
Face'd like a man, though better then his own?
Perfection is in unitie; preferr
One woman first, and then one thing in her.          10
I, when I value gold, may think upon
The ductilness, the application,
The wholsomness, the ingenuitie,
From rust, from soil, from fire ever free:
But if I love it, 'tis because 'tis made          15
By our new nature (Use) the soule of trade.
   All these in women we might think upon
(If women had them) and yet love but one.
Can men more injure women then to say
They love them for that, by which they're not they?          20
Makes virtue woman? must I cool my bloud
Till I both be, and find one wise and good?
May barren Angels love so. But if we
Make love to woman; Vertue is not she:
As Beauty is not nor wealth. He that strayes thus          25
From her to hers, is more adulterous
Then if he took her maid. Search every sphear

And firmament, our *Cupid* is not there:
He's an infernal god and under ground,
With *Pluto* dwells, where gold and fire abound;                30
Men to such Gods, their sacrificing Coles
Did not in Altars lay, but pits and holes:
Although we see Celestial bodies move
Above the earth, the earth we Till and love:
So we her ayres contemplate, words and heart,                  35
And virtues; but we love the Centrique part.
    Nor is the soul more worthy, or more fit
For love, then this, as infinit as it.[1]

"Loves Progress" is one of the indelicate, extravagant compositions of the younger Donne. Its first section is quoted here because
it illustrates the effect of intense training in logic and rhetoric upon
literary style and taste.

The poem is an example of Donne's delight in the calculated
abuse of prescribed formulae; it is a string of those "illaqueations
of sophisms" and "juggleries of words" that irritated Sir Francis
Bacon. The main argument urges that the true lover must advance
his cause by kissing, not his mistress' lips, but her feet. This
approach is not recommended in order that the lover may win
his mistress through abject devotion—Donne has no patience with
such romantic, symbolic posturing. On the contrary, he reasons
that the lover's purpose is physical conquest, and that, therefore,
the road from the feet up is a more direct route to the woman's
sexual parts than the way from her lips down. The title receives
literal explication in the poem: Only the lover who begins at the
feet can claim to make progress—he who starts at the lips must
descend. This risqué version of Ovidian counsel in the art of love
consists of three parts: the first proposes the end of love (lines
1–37); the second (lines 38–72) satirizes the conventional approach
("But in attaining this desired place/How much they erre; that
set out at the face"); the third part (lines 73–96) argues in favor
of the opposite starting point ("Rather set out below; practice my
art").

Donne begins with a variation on the Aristotelian axiom that
all created things strive towards their proper end. This is the course
ordained by nature; whenever nature's end is frustrated, the result
is unnatural. Hence, to enforce the point, lines 4–8 give several

examples of monstrosity. The second proposition, "Perfection is in unitie" (line 8), echoes Aristotle's *esse est componi et unum esse,* "to be is to be unified and to be one" (*Metaphysics,* 8.10). Any thing divided into parts cannot attain perfection; perfect being, which is God, is whole and indivisible. At this point Donne practices his first deceit through words. Translating "unitie" as *singularity,* he advances to his definition of the end of love: "preferr/One woman first, and then one thing in her."

So far, the poet has followed the method prescribed in his logic textbook by beginning with general axioms and stating his definition. The latter, also according to the rules, consists of *genus* and *differentia:*

> A Perfecte Definition setting foorth of a thing, is that, which is made of the whole kinde or general, and the proper difference of that severall sort which is defined, where the first part is called the generall, the other the proper or speciall difference . . . So the Church is a number of men in Christ Jesus, where *A number of men is the general, and in Christ Jesus, is the proper difference.*[2]

Donne's witty definition, however, consists of a *genus* and a *differentia* in the most literal sense: The general is a member of woman*kind,* and the difference is her specific sexual difference from the male.

Having set down his definition, the writer should prove its applicability. The most cogent proofs were those that argued from the causes, of which there were four: the efficient, material, formal, and final cause; and "no man is saide to knowe anye thing thoroughly afore he know the causes thereof."[3] The division into causes applies to any matter whatsoever: For building a house one needs a builder (efficient cause), wood and stone (material cause), functional shape of walls and roof (formal cause), in order to find shelter in it (final cause). Donne argues that in the art of love the efficient cause is the lover, the material the woman's body, the formal her sexual parts, and the final cause sexual intercourse. Lines 11–36 are a series of deft maneuvers to prove that the woman's sexual difference from the male is indeed the formal cause. The formal was of all causes the most important: "The forme is a cause, by the which a thing is that which it is; and so differeth from all other things."[4] The true lover who seeks the right end of love must therefore precisely understand what makes his mistress different from other objects.

The poet accuses men who love a woman for reasons other than her sex of both fallacy and folly. Their error lies in their mistaking an adjunct for a formal cause. It is at this point that the argument increases in ingenuity. Adjuncts are characteristics or qualities of a subject. They are either *common* or *proper,* and each of these two kinds is further subdivided into *separable* and *inseparable.* Common adjuncts are those shared by several subjects; eating, drinking, and sleeping, for example, are common to man and beast, and cannot be separated from them; on the other hand, riches, poverty, and sickness may be common to good and evil men, but they can also be separated from either. Proper adjuncts are always joined to one and the same subject: It is the proper and inseparable adjunct of a body to be seen and felt; but, although it was Adam's proper adjunct to live in Paradise (since no other man ever lived there), it was also, unfortunately, separable from him. Donne uses the division and subdivision of adjuncts in lines 11–17. He proves, with a logical sleight of hand, that the virtue of a woman cannot be her formal cause. All her good qualities are merely adjuncts. Moreover, they are not *proper* to her: "the ductilness, the application,/ The wholsomness, the ingenuitie," and purity are aspects common both to her and to gold. (The deliberate sophism here is in glossing over the ambiguity of the language: "ductilness," "application," and so on apply literally to gold but only figuratively to woman.) But, Donne continues, at least in gold these common adjuncts are *inseparable,* but they are decidedly *separable* from womanhood: "(If women had them)." Consequently, "Can men more injure women than to say / They love them for that, by which they're not they?" The same argument applies to the love of the mistress for her virtue, beauty, and wealth. These attributes are also neither *proper* nor *inseparable* but merely ancillary. Hence, whoever loves her for such qualities "is more adulterous / Then if he took her maid." Why *more* adulterous? The answer follows logically from the definition in lines 9–10. He who redirects his ardor from mistress to maid at least regards the "true end" of love; he may have changed from one member of the *genus* to another, but he is still intent on the *differentia,* the vagina, and therefore respects the formal cause of womanhood. The lover who is so dimwitted that he mistakes a common and separable quality in his mistress for a formal cause has strayed much further into error.

Donne's most ribald statement in the poem occurs in lines 35–38. He has just said that we contemplate the macrocosm of the heavens but love and work its center, the earth. In the contemporary drawings that visually sought to prove the correspondence between the microcosm of the body and the large world of God, the proportions of the human being and their macrocosmic equivalents were measured in terms of the circle. The circle drawn around the human figure sometimes had as its center the sexual organs. Donne abstracts from this the following sophistic conclusion: If the earth is the macrocosmic center and the sexual organ the corresponding center of the world of the body, then a woman's sex is the only solid, earthly thing about her; all her other possessions, "words and heart, / And virtues," are what some may call heavenly, although Donne prefers to pun on them as "ayres." The woman's sex is a microcosm in the macrocosm of her person, as the earth is a little world in the large world of the heavens. The earth and the vagina therefore correspond; if the former is circular, so is the latter. The circle, as everyone knows, is the symbol of infinity and perfection, and Donne, again treating a figure literally, concludes that whatever is circular is infinite and perfect. Hence, "Nor is the soul more worthy, or more fit / For love, then this [the vagina], as infinit as it."

This ends the first part of "Loves Progress." The poet has finished the defense of his definition by rapidly moving from one fallacy to another. Besides the fallacies and verbal tricks already pointed out, Donne's contemporaries would be quick to notice the first fallacy from which all the others proceed: the neglect of the distinction between two kinds of final causes. One final cause may be the nature of the thing considered, another the purpose of the agent: A house is built to live in (its inherent purpose) although the builder erects it to make a living (the agent's purpose). A like distinction can be made in the case of love: The end of love, according to such a popular Renaissance handbook as Castiglione's *The Courtier,* is the perfection of the lovers; however, the end of some lovers is copulation. Donne mixes the two kinds of final causes. Put into syllogistic form, his fallacious argument runs:

> the end of love is perfection;
> the end of my love is copulation;
> therefore, copulation is perfection.

It is sometimes thought that Donne's ingenious and satirical performances were meant to disparage the customary academic knowledge of the age. Yet the degree to which he abuses official norms and methods in such an early poem as "Loves Progress" is no proof of scepticism on his part, nor of an inclination to discard received tradition. University graduates or the aristocrats who had spent a few 'finishing' years at Oxford or Cambridge were quite familiar with the deliberately perverse approach to established views. Satire on, and parody of, scholastic training had been incorporated into university ceremonial; Donne's "Loves Progress" is very much like the *Praevaricatio* or 'varier's speech' that was part of the official disputation.

Commencement disputation was an elaborate affair, beginning with the stately entrance of its participants—the moderator, the defendant, his 'father,' or sponsor, and his opponents. After a series of formal gestures the moderator said a prayer and followed it with his opening address, which explained the question to be debated. The 'father' then introduced his 'son,' who would eventually have to answer the question. However, the father first gave the topic further preliminary treatment. At this point, the *praevaricator* or 'varier' appeared on the scene to give his approach to the matter; his version was expected to be humorous and was, in fact, often satirical, if not sarcastic or risqué. Next, the father called upon the son to state his position vis-à-vis the proposed question. The student, after an invocation for divine guidance, gave a brief exposition of his stand; meanwhile, the beadles went around the audience to hand out copies of the defendant's Latin verse composition on the subject. The father engaged the defendant in some friendly maneuvering but soon made room for the first official opponent, and the syllogistic wrangling began in earnest.[5]

The brief exposé of a full-dress disputation is relevant at this point for two reasons. First, Donne was not original in attacking scholastic learning. He did not, in fact, attack it; he used it wittily, after the manner of the *praevaricator*, and such use, or abuse, of it went back to the days of the medieval schools. Secondly, and more importantly, if we remember that the commencement disputations were the most elaborate of many such debates that the student attended or participated in during his college years, we can account, at least in part, for the disputatious tone not only of Donne but of many other seventeenth-century authors.

All parts of the curriculum trained the student in argumentation. If the disputation was designed to show his adroitness in syllogistic debate, the declamations which he had to deliver were no less dialectical: One point was nearly always opposed to another. Milton's *Prolusions* are the best-known examples of the undergraduate declamatory style. The "First Prolusion" argues that Day is more excellent than Night; the second, although its title, "On the Harmony of the Spheres," does not announce a polemic, defends the concept of universal harmony against Aristotle's doubts about it; all the *Prolusions* are structured around a similar antithesis.

The rhetorical compositions written by the student for his tutor were almost always on topics that left room for the marshalling of arguments pro and con. Classical subjects were popular, not only because with the classics the scholar was on home ground, but also because the evidence on many facts of ancient history was often inconclusive and therefore debatable. In his very best Latin a student would render a verdict, for example, on whether or not Alexander, or Aristotle, committed suicide; whether Penelope was adulterous or not; whether Homer's blindness was real or a later fiction; and even whether or not the Greeks really did capture Troy.[6]

The seventeenth-century tendency to oppose points of view was ingrained and is a distinct feature of the literature of the age. Attitudes contrary to one's own are frequently included in order to be rejected. It is an obvious trick of style in Bacon: "For the end of logic is to teach a form of argument to secure reason, and not to entrap it; the end likewise of moral philosophy is to procure the affections to fight on the side of reason, and not to invade it; the end of rhetoric is to fill the imagination with observations and images, to second reason, and not to oppress it." [7] This passage is an extreme example of what others did less tersely. Sir Thomas Browne describes, in the apparently wandering first paragraph of the *Religio Medici,* his religious affiliation. He declares that he is an upright Christian, but he simultaneously disposes of all the arguments that may be brought against his sincerity. He not merely states his faith; he also, with considerable agility, abolishes any adverse criticisms by introducing and rejecting them *en passant.* The disputatious style of his prose is noticeable in the phrases *though, yet, not that, but, neither, rather:*

> For my Religion, though there be severall circumstances that might perswade the world I have none at all, as the generall scandall of my profession, the naturall course of my studies, the indifferency of my behaviour, and discourse in matters of Religion, neither violently defending one, nor with that common ardour and contention opposing another; yet in despight hereof I dare, without usurpation, assume the honorable stile of a Christian: not that I merely owe this title to the Font, my education, or Clime wherein I was borne, as being bred up either to confirme those principles my Parents instilled into my unwary understanding; or by a generall consent proceed in the Religion of my Countrey: But that having, in my riper yeares, and confirmed judgement, seene and examined all, I finde myselfe obliged by the principles of Grace, and the Law of mine owne reason, to embrace no other name but this; neither doth herein my zeale so farre make me forget the generall charitie I owe unto humanity, as rather to hate then pity Turkes, Infidels, and (what is worse) the Jewes, rather contenting my selfe to enjoy that happy stile, then maligning those who refuse so glorious a title.

The vogue of framing a composition by the inclusion of attitudes contrary to one's own was not restricted to prose. Many of the best-known poems illustrate the fashion. Donne's "A Valediction: forbidding Mourning" contrasts dross, sublunary love with his refined ideal. Forbidding his beloved to mourn is no mere admonition; he works his way through a series of 'logical' steps to prove that his intended voyage assures their Love. Were it not for his temporary removal from her, they would never know the perfection of their spiritual bond. Leaving in order to return, he will describe a circle around her, but he can only do this if she remains firm instead of weakly dissolving into tears:

> Thy firmnes makes my circle just
> And makes me end, where I begunne.

When the voyage becomes a circle around her, it will be a symbolic proof of the infinity and perfection of their mutual love. Thus his travel furnishes a manifest assurance of their devotion to each other, and the beloved is expressly forbidden to mourn.

Another well-known example of Donne's controversial contriving is "The Canonization," in which an imagined opponent is first silenced by being granted every point in his case (the lover's old age, ruined fortune, lack of career, and the inefficacy of love), and then demolished by arguments in defense of the holiness of passion.[8]

Controversy is also the reason for the formal ordering of Marvell's *"To his Coy Mistress."*[9] The speaker recognizes the other point of view: "Had we but World enough, and Time, / This coyness Lady were no crime." He then counters with "But at my back I alwaies hear/ Times winged Charriot hurrying near," and hence forcefully concludes: "Now therefore, . . . let us sport us . . . ." We ought not to suppose that Marvell and other metaphysicals learned this kind of tight, logical structure from Donne.[10] Its origin is not so narrowly definable as all that. The writers' preference for the antithetical disposition of their matter is traceable to their schooldays.

## Paradise Lost: *consequential contrasts*

We ought to remember that "composition" carried its precise etymological meaning; it meant a putting together, or careful fitting of independent parts. Jonson only summarizes current usage when he says:

> *For* a man to write well, there are required three Necessaries. To read the best Authors, observe the best Speakers: and much exercise of his owne style. In style to consider, what ought to be written; and after what manner; Hee must first thinke, and excogitate his matter; then choose his words, and examine the weight of either. Then take care in placing, and ranking both matter and words, that the composition be comely; and to doe this with diligence, and often.

In the framing of a composition the important parts were often arranged in contrast. Donne, for example, intended to write a series of annual poems to commemorate the death of his patron's daughter, Elizabeth Drury. He wrote, however, only two such *Anniversaries*. We find the reason for there being only two if we look upon them as companion pieces; the second, which celebrates the joy of heaven, answers the first, which laments the little girl's loss to the world. Together the poems form one composition in two parts that are contrasts in argument, belief, and mood.

A like relationship exists between Browne's *Urne-Buriall* and *The Garden of Cyrus*. These discursive treatises, filled with antiquarian and curious, pedantic lore, were properly understood only when modern critics read them in conjunction. They are, in fact, a stylized debate on life and death, debating the empty values of this world in contrast to the riches of the next. Professor F. L. Huntley's brilliant exposition of their structure proves that they are companion pieces, *Urne-Buriall* dealing with death, ignorance and darkness, *The Garden* with life, knowledge, and light.[11]

Milton's "L'Allegro" and "Il Penseroso" are evidently parallel poems indebted to the student's declamation. Comus' epicurean advocacy of the use of nature's abundance against the Lady's platonic defense of her virginal Ideal is more than reminiscent of academic debate, as is the argument between the brothers on the power of chastity, arbitrated by the attendant Spirit. "Lycidas," too, is based on antithesis: Its three main parts—the lament for Lycidas as shepherd-poet and as shepherd-priest, and his apotheosis—are variations on the opposition between a desire for worldly fame and the acceptance of the will and reward of heaven.

This tendency of the mind to define one idea in contrast to another, a habit which Milton shares with his contemporaries, is important for an unbiased understanding of *Paradise Lost*. Milton has been accused of a 'puritanical' reaction to those efforts with which man has sought to relieve his condition since the Fall: the riches of classical culture, the conclusions of science, the monuments of architecture, and even the passionate attachment to a beloved. Mundane readers find the spiritual values Milton defends less attractive than the worldliness he supposedly rejects. But Milton wished to write a Christian epic with a new kind of hero, a man in service to a new ideal, and he was intent on *demonstrating* the pre-eminence of his views by comparing them to all previous conceptions of heroic conduct. If his heroism is "the better forti-tude/ Of Patience and Heroic Martyrdom," as yet "unsung," he must *prove* it to be superior to the official, traditional versions of heroism of the past. He therefore introduces the devil as a parody of the ancient hero. The Satan of Books I and II is at first vaguely reminiscent of the noble aspirations of the Homeric and Virgilian worlds. He has an undeniable grandeur, both in stature and in the range and intensity of his emotional response. Yet after Milton takes the reader up to heaven in Book III and shows him the contrast between God's Council and hell's Parliament, between the Son's obedient love and Satan's willful pride, the poet might expect any of his contemporaries to perceive that *Paradise Lost* is an *argumentative* justification of the will of God and that Satan gets the worst of the argument.

As Milton continues to enlighten the reader on what man's ideal conduct should be, past norms are shown to be increasingly unsatisfactory. Satan grows smaller when we see him in Eden as he approaches the first man who will eventually learn to model himself after the suffering Christ. And in the middle of *Paradise Lost* the Prince of all the Rebel Powers becomes a grotesque caricature of the primitive hero relying on force.

Milton's epic is a series of such contrasts. If the "paradise within" is the real battlefield, all other wars, waged with material weapons, are mere skirmishes without a decisive outcome; they are continued until the divine will puts an end to their folly. If "th'upright heart and pure" is the temple of the Spirit, any material temple is but a nine-days wonder and an imperfect imitation of infernal enterprise:

> . . . And here let those
> Who boast in mortal things, and wondring tell
> Of *Babel,* and the works of *Memphian* Kings
> Learn how thir greatest Monuments of Fame,
> And Strength and Art are easily outdone
> By Spirits reprobate, and in an hour
> What in an age they with incessant toyl
> And hands innumerable scarce perform.
>
> I, 692–699

If a living faith in God is the true source of Christian joy, the occupations of the civilized ancients are but vanity. They are disposed of in Book II, when the fallen Angels pass their time in hell with Olympic games, imperfectly harmonious music, and the discussion of perplexing philosophical dilemmas. If knowledge of God is the highest end of man's searching, the intricacies of stellar and planetary motions are a negligible object of concern for men on earth:

> . . . if they list to try
> Conjecture, he his Fabric of the Heav'ns
> Hath left to thir disputes, perhaps to move
> His laughter at thir quaint Opinions wide
> Hereafter . . . .

VIII, 75–79

Finally, if the love of God is Adam's dearest possession, the love of woman cannot replace it.

The antithetical arrangement of the matter in *Paradise Lost* is reminiscent of the polemic practice that Milton had been taught at St. Paul's and Cambridge and had fully mastered by composing an impressive sequence of pamphlets between 1642 and 1655. *Paradise Lost* is contrived to glorify an ideal. Whatever differs from that view is manipulated by Milton in such a way that the difference becomes an inferior contrast. He does not hesitate to use the debater's technique of ridicule and generalization: All that is not God, is against God; all that is not noble to the poet, is ignoble; all knowledge not founded on faith is the vanity of human wishes. Satan's legions in Book I are not only compared to the armies of mythology and pagan antiquity, but also to the Christian armies that defended the faith under Charlemagne, who "with all his Peerage/ Fell by *Fontarabbia*" (I, 586–587). The burlesque of the battle in heaven is meant to make us laugh, not only at Satan and his host, but at the 'might' of the loyal angels as well. Michael's great deed that "deserv'd/ Memorial" (VI, 354–355) is the wound he inflicts on Satan in a grandiose single combat. Yet after the stirring description of that event and the grievousness of the wound, we are coolly informed that Satan merely rearranges his "liquid texture" and goes on fighting.[12]

Anyone who argues that Milton's contrasts are unfair misses the mark altogether. Of course, the trick of heightening the opposition is not 'fair.' Achilles, Odysseus, Aeneas, and Turnus are not Satanic; Satan is not the old epic ideal, but a parody of it. And the works of classical antiquity, with all the achievements of later learning, undeniably enrich the spirit. Yet we must remember that for Milton's age poetry implied a full command of rhetoric, and the poet, like the orator, must "apply and recommend the dictates of reason to imagination, in order to excite the appetite and will." In order to give the audience an appetite for virtue, the poet may use all his rhetorical powers, including generalization, parody, satire, and other means of ridicule and rejection. Milton saw poetry as an alternative to "the office of a pulpit" and, like Dean Donne, tried to rule and direct the emotional response of his audience. We do not literally apply Donne's hyperboles or quick conceits, nor do we judge his passionate harangues by some yardstick of whatever "reality" we may dream ourselves to be living in. Surely we ought to grant Milton the same latitude as well.

There is no warrant for taking opinions expressed in *Paradise Lost* and foisting them on Milton in order to describe either his supposed personality or the opinions of the age. His satire on the reliance on force notwithstanding, Milton was no pacifist. He prided himself on having been a skillful swordsman when he still had the use of his eyes: "I am a man of courage and strength, and in earlier years I learned, through daily practice, how to handle my sword with skill. Commonly armed with this weapon, I used to think myself a match for any man, even one far stronger than myself, and I had no fear of any harm that men can do to one another." [13] His scheme for the education of children recommends their training in the arts of war, and elsewhere he praised Cromwell's exploits on the battlefield. [14] He admired splendid architecture and especially enjoyed the monuments of Florence and Naples. He studied mathematics with zeal during his five years of retirement at Horton and claims that while touring Italy he paid a call on Galileo in his villa outside Florence. Love of antiquity and zeal for learning were so early acquired as to be part of him. Their apparent rejection in *Paradise Lost* and again in *Paradise Regained* is a foil to set off Milton's white Ideal.

## Religio Medici: *Aristotle* versus *Moses*

The interpreter of seventeenth-century literature ought always to heed the likelihood that the structural principle of a work is a contention that plays off one view against another. Donne's picture of the world as dust and ashes in the *First Anniversairie* offers no proof of his disturbed sensibility or of the distemper of his followers; nor ought we to impute a similar unrelieved melancholy to Sir Thomas Browne because of the mournful tone of *Urne-Buriall*. Our interpretation of these works must take into account that they represent only one part of the intellectual inventory of their authors.

Critics no longer deny the antithetical arrangement of the two *Anniversaries* or of *Urne-Buriall* and *The Garden of Cyrus*, but works that are less strikingly bipartite are not always treated with cautious regard for their structure. Such a curious intellect as that of Sir Thomas Browne often tempts the student to quote out of context. The facets and odd interests of that eccentric mind are so varied that one can illustrate many vagaries of seventeenth-century opinion by combing Browne's works for a fitting quotation. The historian of ideas who wishes to trace such popular topics as the rise of science, of scepticism, of new attitudes towards language, logic, and rhetoric—not to speak of the 'dissociation of sensibility'—can nearly always rely on Browne to provide him with a signpost to one or another direction. That private memorial, the *Religio Medici*, is especially fertile. It is assumed to have been a private document not seriously intended for publication, an impression that is reinforced by Browne's apparently rambling discourse. Yet here too, one notices a constant opposition.

Borrowing one of Browne's own metaphors, one may say that two names appear so frequently in the *Religio Medici* as to be woven into the fabric of that work: The one is Aristotle, the other Moses. Aristotle is throughout afforded little praise. He was the first great empiricist, riveting his attention on the known world. He attempted to increase human knowledge by human means, an effort of which Browne is rather sceptical. Browne's Aristotle is lacking in 'divinity,' or theology; devoting insufficient attention to God as the first cause, he "left behinde him an imperfect piece of Philosophy" (I, 14).[15] He could not provide answers in theology: "That there is but one world is a conclusion of faith: *Aristotle* with all his Philosophy hath not been able to prove it, and as weakely that the world was eternall" (I, 35). Browne always stresses the limited value of Aristotle's work: On the immortality of the soul all we have is "not a negative from *Aristotle*" (I, 36). Aristotle's limitations were due to his being earthbound so that in higher spheres the rules of his philosophy must be suspended: "I grant that two bodies placed beyond the tenth Spheare, or in a vacuity, according to *Aristotles* Philosophy, could not behold each other," but, Browne goes on to say, in the celestial realm Aristotle's mechanical "Opticks" will be replaced by a "perfect vision" (I, 41). Aristotle is also blamed for transgressing "the rule of his owne Ethicks" (I, 55). Admittedly, Aristotle's study of the known world occasionally produced results, as evident in his "acute, and singular booke of Physiognomy"; however, Browne finds in this work no mention made of chiromancy, the study of "mysticall lines and figures in our hands" (II, 2)—something of a defect in the light of Browne's love of mystical methods.

Aristotle's narrow perspective, the misdirection of his attention, led to the uncertainty of his philosophy, a doubtfulness to which he himself admitted: "*Aristotle* who understood the uncertainty of knowledge, and confessed so often the reason of man too weak for the workes of nature" (II, 8). Since Aristotle was restricted to the finite world, his liability was the erroneous reason of man: "the Lawes of one doe but condemn the rules of another; as *Aristotle* oft-times the opinions of his predecessours, because though agreeable to reason, yet were not consonant to his owne rules, and the Logicke of his proper principles" (II, 9). Man lives not by logic but by faith: Browne's charity derives from the Christian belief that "he that giveth to the poore lendeth to the Lord"; Aristotle had no such eschatology and hence was "too severe, that will not allow us to bee truely liberal without wealth" (II, 13). In the last section of the *Religio Medici* Browne gives his summation and final rejection of Aristotle: "Aristotle whilst hee labours to refute the Idea's of *Plato,* fals upon one himselfe: for his *summum bonum* is a. *Chimaera,* and there is no such thing as his Felicity" (II, 15).

Standing in diameter to Aristotle is Moses, who rightly understands God's design. He is, first of all, God's interpreter: *"I am that I am,* was his owne definition unto *Moses"* (I, 11). Man cannot attain to the illumination granted to Moses, for "our understanding is dimmer than *Moses* Eye" (I, 13). Finite reason abdicates before Moses; in I, 19, Browne marshals empirical arguments that might explain the miracles of the Old Testament, only to conclude that the question "where was then the miracle in the dayes of *Moses?*" is a *quere* made by the devil. The work of Moses has withstood "the teeth of time," in contrast with the sublunary efforts of others: "There were divers that wrote before *Moses,* who notwithstanding have suffered the common fate of time" (I, 23). The authorship of the first five books of the Bible, the *Pentateuch,* was traditionally ascribed to Moses. Since the account of his death occurs in the last book of the Pentateuch (Deut. 34:7), Moses was assumed to have recorded his own death. Browne observes that "some have been of my opinion, and endeavoured to write the history of their own lives; wherein *Moses* hath outgone them all, and left not onely the story of his life, but as some will have it of his death also" (I, 25). It is interesting and significant that the private 'memoriall' which Browne is writing is a genre that he traces to Moses. In the latter Browne finds 'intimations of immortality,' for Moses is not restricted to the visible world: "though there bee but one world to the sense, there are two to reason, the one visible, the other invisible, whereof *Moses* seems to have left description, and of the other so obscurely, that some parts thereof are yet in controversie" (I, 34). Whereas Aristotle could not prove that the world is eternal, "Moses hath decided that question, and all is salved with the new terme of a creation" (I, 35). The only error committed by Moses is that of misdirected empiricism: He desired to see God with "these eyes of flesh"; and the error is all the more surprising in the light of his having been "bred up in all the learning of the *Egyptians*" (I, 41). The education Moses received is the aspect Browne emphasizes more than any other. He will allow "those allegorical interpretations of Scripture" because he believes them to be the result of the "mysticall method of *Moses* bred up in the Hieroglyphicall Schooles of the *Egyptians*" (I, 34). Since the Egyptians were "addicted to those abstruse and mysticall sciences" (II, 2), Moses had learned from them to see this world but as a hieroglyph or 'counterfeit presentment' of another.

Even a casual accumulation of Browne's references to Aristotle and Moses suggests that in the structure of the *Religio Medici* both men are not just historical figures: Each has become an archetype, in the pre-Jungian, Augustinian sense of 'archetype' as paradigm.

Aristotle is the image of man viewing the world with "these eyes of flesh," Moses the image of man living *sub specie aeternitatis*. Suggestion turns into conviction upon the discovery of another distinction in the *Religio Medici*, the patterned contrast between language and reality. Browne associates Aristotle with the metaphysical definitions of scholasticism that attempt to catch reality in language. Moses, however, belongs to the tradition also represented by Hermes Trismegistus, Pythagoras, and Plato. That tradition recognizes reality as boundless and ineffable and approaches it by means of a different and mystical method.

The *Religio Medici* is shot through with phrases, images, and *exempla* that emphasize the problem of meaning. Early in his essay Browne announces that "the *name* of a Christian is become too generall to expresse our faith" (I, 2). Language obscures reality; man speaks of fortune and the work of nature, thereby forgetting that both are the 'hand' of God: "These must not therefore be *named* the effects of fortune, but in a relative way, and as we *terme* the workes of Nature. It was the ignorance of man's reason that begat this very *name*, and by a careless *terme* miscalled the providence of God" (I, 18). That fearful Puritan doctrine of predestination is only the result of man's failure to distinguish between language and reality; there is no present, past, and future in God, no grammatical "distinction of Tenses"; hence predestination is merely a "terrible *terme*" (I, 11). When Browne (in I, 22) comes to speak of points in which he sees "no consequence," all the instances he gives relate to the problem of meaning. Browne finds it ill-advised to prove the existence of the Trinity from God's plural *faciamus hominem;* the plural here is an instance of *pluralis majestatis* and a mere manner of speech. Similarly, Browne would not infer the obedience of wives to their husbands from Sarah's addressing Abraham as 'Lord'—her 'Lord' was no more than ordinary usage. The existence of guardian angels is not proved from the answer given in Acts, 12:2, by those who refused to believe Peter's escape: *"Tis not he, but his Angel";* Browne argues that in context 'angel' is likely to mean 'messenger.' In every instance the emphasis is on the danger of proceeding by means of words. It is not the points, but rather the arguments, that to Browne are of no consequence. He did believe in the Trinity; he desired woman to be obedient to man: "The whole woman was made for man, but the twelfth part of man for woman" (II, 9); and as for guardian angels: "I would easily beleeve, that not onely whole Countries, but particular persons, have their Tutelary, and Guardian Angels" (I, 33).

Sir Thomas considers himself not misled by language; he is able to distinguish between language and reality and is therefore not "convulst" at the *"name* of death" (I, 38). He has set his sights on heaven—hell no longer has reality and has become a 'term' and a 'name': "that terrible term hath never detained me from sin, nor do I owe one good action to the name thereof" (I, 52). He sometimes confesses himself amazed at the difference between language and reality: Pride is "a vice whose *name* is comprehended in a monosyllable, but in its nature not circumscribed with a world" (II, 8); similarly, "we *terme* sleep a death, and yet it is waking that kills us" (II, 12). Hence, when Browne arrives at his own conclusions, he is aware that their formulation is gratuitous: "doe but abstract from the corpulency of bodies, or resolve things beyond their first matter, and you discover the habitation of Angels, which *if I call* the ubiquitary and omnipresent essence of God, *I hope I shall not offend Divinity"* (I, 35). Arguing that "there is therefore some other hand that twines the thread of life than that of nature," he concludes that "though wee confesse our ignorance, I am sure wee do not erre, *if wee say,* it is the hand of God" (I, 43). The peroration in the final section of the *Religio Medici* again emphasizes the language problem: "That wherein God himselfe is happy, the holy Angels are happy, in whose defect the Devils are unhappy; that *dare I call* happinesse: whatsoever conduceth unto this may with an easie Metaphor deserve that *name;* whatsoever else the world *termes* happiness, is to me a story out of *Pliny,* a tale of *Boccace* or *Malizspini,* an apparition or neat delusion, wherein there is no more happinesse than the *name"* (II, 15).

Browne's distrust of language is evident also in his rejection of 'rhetoric,' again a discipline fathered upon Aristotle. In the *Religio Medici* 'rhetoric' has no other than unpleasant connotations. It appeals to the *profanum vulgus:* "the vulgar whose ears are opener to Rhetorick then Logicke" (I, 5); the arguments of the infidels are "the Rhetorick of Satan" (I, 20); before Browne came to understand the truth of the saying that man is a microcosm, he had thought it "onely a pleasant trope of Rhetorick" (I, 34), that is, he believed it to be no more than a 'terme.' Discussing the theory of the traduction of the soul—according to which the soul is transmitted in the seed of the parents—Browne brushes aside Saint Augustine's theory of the infusion of a separately created soul into each body; Saint Augustine's definition *Creando infunditur, infundendo creatur,* is called a mere "Rhetoricall sentence" and no more than a transposition of words (I, 36). Commenting on the difference between theory and practice, Browne equates theory without practice with rhetoric: "we naturally know what is good, but naturally pursue what is evill: the Rhetoricke wherewith I perswade another cannot perswade my selfe" (I, 55).

The repeated emphasis on the hollowness of terms, names, and rhetoric is therefore not merely casual. It serves a cognitive function because it underlines the poverty of language in dealing with reality. Reality is indivisible and ineffable, for the ultimate reality is God—"wee doe too narrowly define the power of God, restraining it to our own capacities" (I, 27). Hence Browne comments so ironically on those "who have had the honour to be textuarie in Divinity" (I, 50) and on the rabbinical scholars who "contend upon the Letter of the Text" (I, 21).

Opposed to the method of Aristotle and the schools, with its faith in definitions, terms, and rhetoric, is the method of the Egyptians, that of Moses and Hermes, of Pythagoras and Plato, which views this world as a hieroglyph of another, with the consequent emphasis on every detail in this world as a sign of some invisible substance or operation.[16] Browne testifies: "The severer Schooles shall never laugh me out of the Philosophy of *Hermes,* that this visible World is but a picture of the invisible, wherein, as in a pourtract [portrait], things are not truely, but in equivocall shapes, and as they counterfeit some more reall substance in that invisible fabrick" (I, 12).

Sir Thomas Browne admires those who lived before Christ whose faith was based on "mysticall Types" (I, 9). He has "often admired the mysticall way of *Pythagoras,* and the secret Magicke of numbers" (I, 12). Nature is God's "universall and publik Manuscript" (I, 16) and has to be read with attention to its divine source: It contains "mysticall letters" and "common Hieroglyphicks" (I, 16). Through such a reading, philosophy—man's fallible discourse—changes into theology: "Those strange and mysticall transmigrations that I have observed in Silke-wormes, turn'd my philosophy into Divinity" (I, 39), and in the same manner tavern music may become a "Hieroglyphicall and shadowed lesson" of the music of the spheres (II, 9).

Browne delights in contrasting the two methods: definitions and terms on the one hand, secrets, mysteries, metaphors, and allegories on the other. "I have therefore forsaken those strict *definitions* of death . . . and have fram'd one in an *hermeticall* way" (I, 39). The Latin roots of 'define' and 'determine' are *finis* and *terminus,* 'end' and 'limit.' To 'define' and to 'determine' mean, for Browne, to 'put an end to' and to 'limit' what is infinite and limitless; the hieroglyphical method is not so presumptuous. "The deepest mysteries ours [our faith] containes have not only been illustrated, but maintained by syllogisme, and the rule of reason"—here Browne's irony approaches sarcasm. In preference to that curious and vain method, he chooses "to lose myself in a mystery, to pursue my reason to an *oh altitudo*" (I, 9). The "Platonick description" is "easie," and "that *allegorical* description of *Hermes* pleaseth mee beyond all the Metaphysical *definitions* of Divines" (I, 10). Nature he does "not *define* with the Schooles" but presents hieroglyphically as "that straight and regular line" of God's wisdom (I, 16). Natural philosophy, or science, cannot determine the span of life, for its secret is with God: "They that found themselves on the radicall balsome or vitall sulphur of the parts, *determine* not why *Abel* liv'd not so long as *Adam.* There is therefore a *secret* glome or bottome of our dayes" (I, 43). The same contrast is emphasized in his discussion of the last judgment; one cannot "*determine* the day and year of this inevitable time" because one may not "imagine the *secret* communicated to a Rabbi, which God hath denied to his Angels" (I, 46). The contrasts are always variations of the one that exists between the "literall commentators" and the "unspeakable mysteries" (I, 45). On the location of heaven and hell, for example, Browne feels that "to *define* them, or strictly to *determine* what and where they are surpasseth my Divinity" (I, 49). And after enquiring further into his sufferings than their "visible effects," he discovers that they were "the *secret* and dissembled favours of his [God's] affection" (I, 53). His most beautiful *oh altitudo*'s are his descriptions of the attributes of God. They are the only means of adumbrating God, for "to *define* either [God's mercy or His justice] is folly in man and insolency even in the devils" (I, 57). For Browne, whatever is true is mysterious: "There are wonders in *true* affection, it is a body of *Aenigmaes, mysteries,* and *riddles*" (II, 6).

'Mystery' retains for Browne, as it did for Donne, its theological meaning. It signifies a truth beyond the reach of human reason but divinely revealed and hence a part of human knowledge. This helps to explain Browne's admonition that "Beware of Philosophy, is a precept not to be received in too large a sense" (I, 12). The philosophy Browne wants us to be wary of is a philosophy of definitions; such a system is finite, relative to man, like Aristotle's; the latter believed only those things to be true that were "consonant to his owne rules, and the Logicke of his proper principles." There is, however, a "mysterious Philosophy" (I, 38) that begins and ends with 'mystery' as the certitude of divine truth. Moses, Hermes, Pythagoras, and Plato were such 'mysterious' philosophers in pursuit of the invisible truth beyond the visible effects.

Upon analysis, it is clear that the frequent mention of Aristotle and Moses in the *Religio Medici* has a metaphorical dimension. Around the two names Browne structures the opposition between language and reality, between finite reason and the mystery of God. It is also evident that a quotation lifted from the *Religio Medici* cannot be taken as reliable evidence of Browne's commitment to any person or cause. Sir Thomas Browne denigrates Aristotle, logic, and rhetoric in order to celebrate, in contrast, the value of metaphor and the depth of the hieroglyphical method. It does not follow that Browne is anti-Aristotelian or disapproves of logic and rhetoric. Aristotle receives high praise for his teleological and experiential method in *Vulgar Errors,* in which many issues are decided by a neat application of the rules of logic. And anyone who will take the trouble to compare the simplistic language of Browne's private letters with the varying styles of his published works can easily see how carefully Browne clothed his public image in an extravagant but patterned array of rhetorical colors.

## The logical apprehension of mortality

The abuse of logic in "Loves Progress" led us into a consideration of the emphasis on dispute, debate, and controversy in the academic curriculum. We have seen the effect of that education in the seventeenth-century mind's habit of defining one idea in contrast to another, and in the consequent preference for antithesis in the structure of literary art. However, writer and audience were attentive not only to the 'controversial' structure of lengthy compositions such as *Paradise Lost* and *Religio Medici* but also to the purpose of logical arguments in the details of smaller works. Even the lyrical poetry of the period often presents a one-sided debate, an argument in which syllogism, true or false, is used to establish the mood and character of the speaker.

Donne's *Holy Sonnet 6*, sometimes cited as an example of confident hope in eternal life, would have been read by his contemporaries as a cry of anguish. Its logic is a series of false syllogisms, a hopeless argument from a helpless voice. The speaker is determined to defeat his opponent, death, yet with every move he exposes the weakness of his position.

> Death be not proud, though some have called thee
> Mighty and dreadfull, for, thou art not soe,
> For, those, whom thou think'st, thou dost overthrow,
> Die not, poore death, nor yet canst thou kill mee;
> From rest and sleepe, which but thy pictures bee,   5
> Much pleasure, then from thee, much more must flow,
> And soonest our best men with thee doe goe,
> Rest of their bones, and soules deliverie.
> Thou 'art slave to Fate, chance, kings, and desperate men, 10
> And dost with poyson, warre, and sicknesse dwell,
> And poppie, 'or charmes can make us sleepe as well,
> And better then thy stroake; why swell'st thou then?
> One short sleepe past, wee wake eternally,
> And death shall be no more, Death thou shalt die.

The first quatrain states the point to be proved: Life does not end with death. The concluding couplet confirms the speaker's belief in eternal life. The sonnet, then, begins and ends with a point of Christian faith, a variation on the cry of the Apostle Paul: "O Death, where is thy sting? O grave, where is thy victory?" (I Cor. 15:55). Paul's certain hope of heaven is founded on his faith in the risen Christ, Whose triumph over death assures all His followers of their resurrection. There is no arguing with death on any other grounds; it will destroy the flesh, even though it leaves the soul to an afterlife. Although this mortal flesh shall put on incorruptibility at the Last Judgment, there is no escaping the fact that death will kill the only body we now know. If that body is only a wretched bag of bones, our fear of losing it is no less for that. This sheer animal fear causes the speaker to cast about for arguments against death. Had he been able to live by faith alone, he would have written no more than six lines: 1-4, and 13-14. The discrepancy between the opening and conclusion on the one hand, and the intervening arguments on the other, would not have escaped Donne's readers. They would immediately notice that the speaker produces nothing but a tangle of sophisms. His specious reasoning shows his anxiety. He is intent on stripping his opponent of his fearful power to kill. In this one-sided debate his attempt to silence death is actually a desperate effort to silence his own anguish. The stylistic purpose of the vicious logic in this sonnet is, first of all, to dramatize the emotional state of the speaker. At the same time, the sophistry proves the impotence of human reason in the face of death and points to the Christian's only recourse: the hope of heaven founded on faith.

Journalistic interpretation of modern poetry focuses the reader's attention first of all on the associations of words. It is the fashion to delineate the structure of a contemporary poem by tracing patterns in the poet's use of image and symbol. The question of the author's intention often makes no difference to the interpreter: An image not consciously intended must be subconscious, and those critics who are, in Joyce's phrase, "easily befreuded" find such an image all the more relevant *because* it is a slip of the mind. It bears repeating that a seventeenth-century reader used altogether different norms. The poet's art was assumed to be an artificial and conscious composition, and the classroom analysis of a poem demanded of the student that he clarify the precise interrelationship of its parts.

Herbert's devotional poetry, with its many complaints of spiritual torpor, slackness, and sterility, does not, at first glance, invite one to constant intellectual exercise. Herbert has been called a poet of narrow range, but he makes up for this alleged limitation by the intricacy of his art. More than any other poet of the period, he demands exact attention to detail. If we follow him with sufficient care, we soon observe how he turns his expertise in argument to poetic advantage.

### Employment (II)

He that is weary, let him sit.
　　My soul would stirre
And trade in courtesies and wit,
　　Quitting the furre
To cold complexions needing it.

Man is no starre, but a quick coal
　　Of mortall fire:
Who blows it not, nor doth controll
　　A faint desire,
Lets his own ashes choke his soul.

When th'elements did for place contest
　　With him, whose will
Ordain'd the highest to be best;
　　The earth sat still,
And by the others is opprest.

Life is a businesse, not good cheer;
　　Ever in warres.
The sunne still shineth there or here,
　　Whereas the starres
Watch an advantage to appeare.

Oh that I were on Orenge-tree,
　　That busie plant!
Then should I ever laden be,
　　And never want
Some fruit for him that dressed me.

But we are still too young or old;
　　The Man is gone,
Before we do our wares unfold:
　　So we freeze on,
Untill the grave increase our cold.

*Employment* (II) is, like so many poems in *The Temple,* the cry of a dejected soul, but the speaker's dejection and emotional disarray are *proved* by his use of a captious argument. He is tired of vainly attending to the things of the spirit and wishes to leave his pensive solitude, to relax the reins of his soul. A simile starts a process of fallacious reasoning: Man is like "a quick coal/ Of mortal fire." That image leads into a discussion of the correspondences between the macrocosm of the world and the microcosm of man. Of the four elements that compose the physical universe (fire, air, water, and earth), fire is the purest and most mobile, in contrast to earth, the lowest element, which "by the others is opprest." The soul is the noblest part of man's microcosm and should, so the speaker argues, imitate the quickness of fire instead of copying the oppressive immobility of earth. The error in the elaborate comparison is that the soul of man cannot correspond to fire: The latter is physical, the former spiritual. In the orthodox theory of correspondences the physical elements of the universe were analogous to the physical details of the body: Man's flesh corresponded to earth, his humor to water, his blood to air; the macrocosmic fire corresponded to the vegetable, vital, and animal spirits, which served the soul as a means of communication with the body. As the universe of elements was sustained in motion by the divine energy of its Creator, so the body was kept alive by that particle of divinity within it, the soul.[17] To urge, as the speaker does, that the soul must obey the order of nature by copying the continuous movement of the fiery sun is erroneous counsel: The heart, not the soul, was the sun's microcosmic equivalent. Any soul that longs for a mundane career, to "stirre/ And trade in courtesies and wit," refuses to accept its pure spirituality, of which God is both the origin and destination. No wonder, then, that the poem ends on so melancholy a note: "we freeze on,/ Untill the grave increase our cold." The awareness of carnal mortality must needs be an unrelieved misery for a man who ignores the immateriality of his soul. Herbert knows, as well as Donne, how to use a specious argument as an illustration of the infirm "humor" and mental imbalance of his speaker. Appropriately, the next poem in *The Temple* is entitled *Deniall;* it rejects outright the sophistry of *Employment* (II) and explains, in the first three stanzas, the emotional cause of the intellectual error in the preceding poem:

> When my devotions could not pierce
>    Thy silent eares;

Then was my heart broken, as was my verse:
My breast was full of fears
And disorder:

My bent thoughts, like a brittle bow,
Did flie asunder:
Each took his way; some would to pleasures go,
Some to the warres and thunder
Of alarms.

As good go any where, they say,
As to benumme
Both knees and heart, in crying night and day,
*Come, come, my God, O come,*
But no hearing.

Herbert's reliance on his reader's training in the minutiae of logic and debate is evident in many other poems. In *The Quidditie* the title itself is a signpost to the poet's intention.

My God, a verse is not a crown,
No point of honour, or gay suit,
No hawk, or banquet, or renown,
Nor a good sword, nor yet a lute:

It cannot vault, or dance, or play;
It never was in *France* or *Spain;*
Nor can it entertain the day
With my great stable or domain:

It is no office, art, or news,
Nor the Exchange, or busie Hall;
But it is that which while I use
I am with thee, and *most take all.*

In scholastic philosophy *quiditas* is the essence of a thing; in English, it came to stand for any subtle verbal distinction. Both meanings apply in Herbert's poem. The last three words are a "quidditie" in the sense of verbal conceit; *most take all* was a phrase used in gambling, equivalent to our 'winner take all.' At the same time, Herbert articulates the essential difference between *The Quidditie* and the poem that immediately precedes it, *Content.* The latter advanced merely secular arguments for withdrawing from the world, ending with the advice: "He that by seeking hath himself once found,/ Hath ever found a happie fortune." But *The*

*Quidditie* qualifies the conclusion; now the speaker finds the *quiditas* of human happiness in God only.

Herbert's rhetorical and logical training is also evident in his fondness for arranging his poems in pairs. He often indicates this in his titles. *Deniall* is one example; another is *The Reprisall.* One meaning of the latter heading implies that the lyric is a musical *reprise* of the theme of the foregoing poem, *"The Thanksgiving."* The relationship between *H. Baptisme* (I) and (II) is more obvious: The first deals with the doctrine of the sacrament, the second with its specific application to the poet. A similar proportion exists between *The Temper* (I) and (II): The one describes the soul's frequent alternation between heavenly joy and abject loss; the other meditates on a particular instance of such an abrupt change. The two sonnets under the title *Love I* make up one argument. The first is a complaint ending with a question: "Who sings thy praise?" The second is a prayer that finds the answer: "All knees shall bow to thee."

Of the many instances of joined poems in *The Temple* one more should be examined: the relationship between *Church-monuments* and *Church-musick.* Herbert achieves in these two lyrics, with exquisite economy of means, the same end as Donne in the antithetical *Anniversaries* and as Browne in *Urne-Buriall* and *The Garden of Cyrus:* a contrast between darkness and light, earth and heaven, time and eternity. In *Church-monuments,* a somber meditation on the decay of ornate tombs, the speaker learns that his own living body is already a crumbling monument, a grave of ashes. The lesson ends with a warning to avoid the lust of the flesh and all its wanton cravings:

> . . . Mark here below
> How tame these ashes are, how free from lust,
> That thou mayst fit thy self against thy fall.

*Church-monuments* has been used to support the notion that the unpleasant odor of the charnel house permeates the art of the century. Taken out of context, it might indeed constitute evidence that Herbert and his contemporaries were not altogether at ease in the graveyard. But to treat the poem in this way is like speaking in half-finished sentences, for it is only half of Herbert's view of life. Its complement is *Church-musick:*

Sweetest of sweets, I thank you: when displeasure
    Did through my bodie wound my minde,
You took me thence, and in your house of pleasure
    A daintie lodging me assign'd.

Now I in you without a bodie move,
    Rising and falling with your wings:
We both together sweetly live and love,
    Yet say sometimes, *God help poore Kings.*

Comfort, I'le die; for if you poste from me,
    Sure I shall do so, and much more:
But if I travell in your companie,
    You know the way to heavens doore.

We notice first how *Church-musick* differs from its predecessor in design: *Church-monuments* is a solemn meditation on decay; this is a song of happiness, a lyric addressed to a beloved: "Sweetest of sweets, I thank you." The next phrase, "when displeasure/ Did through my bodie wound my minde," sums up the melancholy effect of the speaker's reflections at the tomb. But as the body learned its lesson from the grave, the soul "repairs to her devotion" (*Church-monuments,* line 1) and, taken out of the body, is assigned a "daintie lodging" in God's "house of pleasure." The erotic language of *Church-musick* is very daring. Apart from the connotation of "house of pleasure," the first line of the second stanza is narrowly saved from obscenity by the addition of "without a bodie." "Rising and falling" recalls the bawdy conclusion of Shakespeare's sonnet CLI: "No want of conscience hold it that I call/ Her 'love' for whose dear love I rise and fall." Herbert's *"God help poore Kings"* refers us back to the theme of the previous poem: Kings used to build the grandest mausoleums for their dust. All the speaker now needs is the comfort of God's presence, for if God leaves the soul, man will not only die in the flesh but also lose all the delights of love in heaven.

When we observe the antithesis between the two poems, it is apparent that the grave warning to avoid the lust of the flesh is not the result of an unsettled mind with unhealthy fancies about skulls and bones. Man ought to deny his wanton cravings because the alternative, the love of God, is so much more sweet, dainty, and pleasant, and gives a lasting satisfaction. As with Donne,

Browne, and Milton, we must follow Herbert's rhetorical method of argument: affirmation of the ideal through rejection of its opposite.

Herbert is like Browne in his apprehension of mortality: "marshalling all the horrours, and contemplating the extremities thereof, I finde not any thing therein able to daunt the courage of a man, much lesse a well resolved Christian" (*Religio Medici,* I, 38). There is another passage in the *Religio Medici* that, out of context, might create the impression that the period has a predilection for gruesome fantasy. Browne assures us that *"All flesh is grasse,* is not onely metaphorically, but literally true, for all those creatures which we behold are but the hearbs of the field, digested into flesh in them, or more remotely carnified in our selves" (I, 37). This may sound like a variation on Hamlet's question: "Why may not imagination trace the noble dust of Alexander, till he find it stopping a bung-hole?" Hamlet's cynicism, however, is not eased by hope; Browne's curious fancy, on the other hand, is part of a lengthy discourse on the frailty of this mortal coil. He begins that discussion with "Now, for the wals of flesh, wherein the soule doth seem to be immured before the Resurrection, it is . . . ." The qualifying sentence warns the reader to keep in mind that his flesh is only the outer part of him, and Browne immediately offers a consoling contrast with the reference to the resurrection in the life to come.

If Donne, Herbert, and Browne present us with visions of cadaverous horror, it is usually because the purpose of their argument demands it. Death is a fact of life, but so, for them, is Heaven. The "resolved Christian" must resolve their contrast. The religious writers of the age do not offer the hope of resurrection as some sort of opiate to the people; the horrors of death must be marshalled as well. To avoid their full treatment would have offended the seventeenth-century sense of logical method and proportion.

# Chapter Three

❦

# Derivations and Differences

### The exantlation of the word

The master of the grammar school taught the art of words, "right choice of words being indeed," according to the Reverend Hoole, "the foundation of all eloquence." The earliest training in Latin in the lower forms required the pupils to memorize not only the usual meanings but also the derivations of Latin words. The recommended method was to copy the word, the meaning, and the derivation in a little notebook, which the child was to carry about with him and peruse in idle moments. This was the first step towards a knowledge of the "propriety of words and phrases." In the higher forms, when the study of rhetoric took the place of grammar, the scholar learned to fashion that comeliness and copiousness of style for which the knowledge of synonyms was indispensable. Schoolboys culled the classical authors to "endeavour to gain a copy of good and proper words for expression of one and the same thing . . . and in finding such Synonyma's as these they may be helped as well by Dictionaries as by frequent reading." The possession of 'copy,' or abundance of words, did not give Hoole's scholars license to pile one synonym upon another without discrimination: "when they finde many heaped together, it were not amisse to let them enquire the original out of Rider's Latin *Dictionary* or Becman's *De Originibus Latinae Linguae;* and to consider the *differences* that are between words of the same significa-tion." In their daily classroom analysis of a passage from an ancient author, they were to take special note of "derivations and differences," and so discovered that the distinction between words

apparently synonymous was usually etymological. The schoolmaster's stress on the root of words had its effect on the literary
appreciation of the pupils; they grew fond of etymological puns
and quibbles. The university training in logic only increased the
appetite for all kinds of wordplay: The students' experience in
dispute and debate made them conscious of the multiple meanings
of single words. The readiest way to deflate the sails of one's
opponent was to prove him guilty of the abuse of words:

> Now the fallacies whereby men deceive others, and are deceived
> themselves, the Ancients have divided into Verball and Reall. Of
> the Verball, and such as conclude from mistakes of the word,
> although there be no lesse then six, yet are there but two thereof
> worthy our notation; and unto which the rest may be referred:
> that is the fallacie of Aequivocation and Amphibologie; which
> conclude from the ambiguity of some one word, or the ambiguous
> syntaxis of many put together.[1]

We noted in Chapter Two that Browne uses 'define' and 'determine' with an emphasis on their Latin roots, 'end' and 'limit.'
His contemporaries frequently play on the etymology of the same
words. Milton describes Satan's view of heaven, after the voyage
through chaos, as a place

>          . . . extended wide
> In circuit, undetermind square or round
> With Opal Towrs and Battlements adorn'd
> Of living Sapphire. . . .

II, 1047–1050

The use of "undetermind" undercuts the reliability of the entire
description. It conveys that this view of heaven is mere metaphor,
the poet's accommodation to man's fallen understanding. Milton
conjures up a picture of a walled city that one might 'walk around'
("circuit," from *circum-ire,* 'to go around'). He adds immediately
that heaven is not really like this, for it is "undetermind," which
means, literally, that it has no 'fence' or 'boundary.' No walls exist
because heaven is undetermined or endless space.

Marvell's *The Definition of Love* uses two meanings of the word
'definition.' The first is the one of the logic textbook: a precise
statement summing up the nature of a thing by declaring its *genus*
and *differentia.* The conclusion of the poem gives such a logical
definition in two parts: The speaker's love is "the Conjunction

of the Mind,/ And Opposition of the Stars." But Marvell also uses the etymology of 'definition.' The love between speaker and beloved is perfect; it is so pure that it is without any dross of matter. Their love, therefore, describes the circle of the heaven, and the lovers are fixed at the north and south celestial poles, maintaining between them the order and stability of the world. Because they form the outermost circle of the universe, they may be said to partake of infinity, to have no end, yet their love is also sharply 'defined.' A rigorous limit is imposed on it: They are debarred by fate, the axis of the universe, and their loves "Though infinite can never meet." Paradoxically, their love is finite, 'limited,' *because* infinite, 'unlimited.'[2]

The instances of witty exploration of the several meanings of 'define' and 'determine' warn the modern reader to look for the possibility of multiple meanings elsewhere, or rather everywhere, in the literary art of the period. Titles are often ambiguous. Donne's "Exstasie" means 'exaltation,' but also, literally, 'to stand outside': In the poem the souls of the lovers leave their respective bodies to carry on their debate in animated suspension. "Canonization" means more than 'declaration of holiness.' It is a formal process, involving a debate between a defender of the supposed saint and an opponent known as the devil's advocate. Moreover, it requires proof of saintliness in miracles and evidence of heroic pursuit of virtue on the part of the person to be canonized. All these requirements are met in the poem. The devil's advocate is not heard, but we know him to be present; he is the recipient of the angry lash: "For Godsake, hold your tongue." The third stanza offers the miracle of resurrection performed by the saintly lovers: "Wee dye and rise the same, and prove/ Mysterious by this love." The next stanza shows the lovers' extraordinary devotion to virtue in their total renunciation of the world.

Of the metaphysicals, Herbert is most adept at choosing a title that carries a medley of meanings, each of which is skillfully applied in the text of the poem.[3] *The Agonie* is obviously about the mortal fear suffered by Christ on the Mount of Olives, where He contemplated the horror of His imminent death. Yet originally the Greek word means 'contest' or 'struggle,' and three kinds of contest are developed in the poem: the struggle between Christ's fear of suffering and His desire to do the will of His Father; the

conflict between the sin of man and the love of God; the clash
between worldly knowledge and divine wisdom.

> Philosophers have measur'd mountains,
> Fathom'd the depths of seas, of states, and kings,
> Walk'd with a staffe to heav'n, and traced fountains:
>     But there are two vast, spacious things,
> The which to measure it doth more behove:
> Yet few there are that sound them; Sinne and Love.
>
> Who would know Sinne, let him repair
> Unto Mount Olivet; there shall he see
> A man so wrung with pains, that all his hair,
>     His skinne, his garments bloudie be.
> Sinne is that presse and vice, which forceth pain
> To hunt his cruell food through ev'ry vein.
>
> Who knows not Love, let him assay
> And taste that juice, which on the crosse a pike
> Did set again abroach; then let him say
>     If ever he did taste the like.
> Love is that liquour sweet and most divine,
> Which my God feels as bloud; but I, as wine.

The title of *Divinitie* puns on 'theology' and 'conjecture.' In
*Unkindnesse,* the speaker describes himself as both 'unfriendly' and
'unnatural' because, as God's child, his lack of filial love is a
deviation from the normal behavior in man*kind. The Temper* (I)
applies four contemporary meanings of 'temper.' The first is 'a
proportionate arrangement of parts': "Wilt thou meet arms with
man, that thou dost stretch/ A crumme of dust from heav'n to
hell?" The second meaning is 'mental composure' or 'evenness of
disposition': The speaker would be happy "If what my soul doth
feel sometimes/ My soul might ever feel." The third sense is the
temper or hardness of steel: "how should my rymes/ Gladly
engrave thy love in steel." Lastly, we have a musical reference;
tuning an instrument also used to be called 'tempering': "This
is but tuning of my breast,/ To make the musick better."
    Herbert plays similarly with the heading of *Mans Medley.* The
poem begins with the use of medley in the musical sense: a
composition combining incongruous parts or subjects. Birds have
their reason for singing, but when the poet 'measures' human

pleasure—that is, calculates *and* gives rhythmical expression to the joy of man—it appears that man's delight consists of two incongruous parts:

> Heark, how the birds do sing,
>     And woods do ring.
> All creatures have their joy: and man hath his.
>     Yet if we rightly measure,
>         Mans joy and pleasure
> Rather hereafter, then in present, is.

Human joy is like a musical medley because man is a medley in a larger sense; he is a mixture of heterogeneous substances, one earthly, the other heavenly:

> To this life things of sense
>     Make their pretence:
> In th' other Angels have a right by birth:
>     Man ties them both alone,
>         And makes them one,
> With th' one hand touching heav'n, with th' other earth.

In the next stanza, the sense of 'medley' changes again, as Herbert focuses on a specialized meaning of the word: a 'medley' was also a costume of variegated parts or colors (the 'motley' of Shakespeare's fools, or the patched-up habit of Chaucer's sergeant of the law, who "rood but hoomly in a medlee coote"):

> He wears a stuffe whose thread is course and round,
>     But trimm'd with curious lace,
>         And should take place
> After the trimming, not the stuffe and ground.

The title *The Storm* means 'atmospheric disturbance' in the first two lines ("If as the windes and waters here below/ Do flie and flow"), but a little later it refers to a military attack on a fortification ("Mounting more and more/ Dares to assault thee, and besiege thy doore").

*The Size* opens with "Content thee greedie heart," and Herbert applies here the special Cambridge use of 'size'—the portion allowed to students at meals. Man must be content with a modest portion of joy in life in order to have an abundance of delight in Heaven; the reason: "To be in both worlds full/ Is more then

God was, who was hungrie here." A few stanzas later the speaker
argues that the Christian's size or 'portion' of pleasure should
correspond to the size or 'dimension' of his body.

> A Christians state and case
> Is not a corpulent, but a thinne and spare,
> Yet active strength: whose long and bonie face
>     Content and care
>     Do seem to equally divide,
>     Like a pretender, not a bride.

The examples given so far—and many more could be added—
illustrate Herbert's quick shifting among varied meanings of a
word. However, he sometimes selects only one meaning, but then
employs it in such a way that his chosen interpretation of that
word determines the argument, the attitude, and the character
of the speaker. *Redemption,* one of the early sonnets in *The Temple,*
shows this typically Herbertian technique. The poem is an allegory
on the exchange of Testaments, the Old for the New, through the
sacrifice of Christ. A sonnet is normally lyrical, but the language
of this particular one is surprisingly cold and legalistic in its
rendering of God's death for the sake of life in man.

> Having been tenant long to a rich Lord,
>     Not thriving, I resolved to be bold,
>     And make a suit unto him, to afford
> A new small-rented lease, and cancell th' old.
> In heaven at his manour I him sought:
>     They told me there, that he was lately gone
>     About some land, which he had dearly bought
> Long since on earth, to take possession.
> I straight return'd, and knowing his great birth,
>     Sought him accordingly in great resorts;
>     In cities, theatres, gardens, parks, and courts:
> At length I heard a ragged noise and mirth
>     Of theeves and murderers: there I him espied,
>     Who straight, *Your suit is granted,* said, & died.

The contrast between the subject of the poem—the mystery of
Christ's redemptive sacrifice—and the curiously unemotional style
originates in Herbert's etymological interpretation of the title:
'Redemption' is derived from the Latin *redimere,* 'to buy back.'[4]
The speaker is a man who wishes to negotiate the cancellation

of his old lease in order to buy another on easier ("small-rented") terms. This concern for business makes him incapable of comprehending God's design. The speaker views God as a rich lord, like himself preoccupied with buying and selling. Of course, he seeks Christ in the wrong places. Having found Him, quite by accident, he records only what is of interest to himself: His suit was granted. He makes no mention of the divine suffering; he shows no feeling of compassion, not even any evidence of surprise. There is no better way in which Herbert could have illustrated simultaneously the incomprehensibility of the measureless love that causes God to die for man, and man's unworthiness of that sacrifice because of the self-seeking meanness of his spirit.

One meaning of the title of *Businesse* is 'diligence.' The poem is addressed to an idle, sinful soul who neglects all occasion for repentance. The speaker exhorts the soul to 'get busy' and attend to its salvation. Yet a soul in a state of sin is cut off from the spiritual life. Mired in the flesh, how can it understand a spiritual argument if all its concerns are material? The only solution is for the speaker to present his case in terms a materialist understands. Herbert therefore focuses on the other meaning of 'businesse': His speaker tries to convince the soul that the avoidance of sin is an advantageous commercial transaction. He repeatedly uses the language of the accountant: "Lesser pains [in life] scape greater ones" [in hell]; if Christ's triumph over death had not regained eternal life, then "two deaths had been thy fee." Should the soul neglect redemptive grace, it will live in misery both on earth and in hell; that would indeed be a bad casting of accounts because, in that case, "Two lives worse then ten deaths be." Finally, the materialist is made to see the possibility of loss and gain in terms of those metals so precious to him, gold and silver:

> He that loseth gold, though drosse,
> Tells to all he meets, his crosse:
> He that sinnes, hath he no losse?
>
> He that findes a silver vein,
> Thinks on it, and thinks again:
> Brings thy Saviours death no gain?

*Dialogue,* which follows *Businesse,* continues to focus on the imagery of bargaining. Now the crass soul argues with God, advancing, in order to refuse God's offer of gain, the most presumptuous of arguments, namely, its inability to pay in kind:

> Sweetest Saviour, if my soul
> > Were but worth the having,
> Quickly should I then controll
> > Any thought of waving.
> But when all my care and pains
> Cannot give the name of gains
> To thy wretch so full of stains,
> What delight or hope remains?

God corrects the soul's presumption. Using a diction that this materialist cannot fail to understand, God speaks like a shopkeeper with an eye on the scale:

> *What, Child, is the ballance thine,*
> > *Thine the poise and measure?*
> *If I say, Thou shalt be mine;*
> > *Finger not my treasure.*
> *What the gains in having thee*
> *Do amount to, only he,*
> *Who for man was sold, can see;*
> *That transferr'd th' accounts to me.*

Only God determines the amount of gain. He alone knows the worth of man because He paid the price of sale. Although the soul sees "no merit, leading to this favour," it reluctantly surrenders: "Sinne disclaims and I resigne." The soul means that it will resign itself to the divine plan. At this point, Herbert's God proves His skill in distinguishing between the varied senses of a word; He implies that "I resigne" may mean 'I resign myself to,' but also 'I resign from.' Only the latter meaning will suffice for God, who Himself resigned from Heaven to become man:

> *That is all, if that I could*
> > *Get without repining;*
> *And my clay, my creature, would*
> > *Follow my resigning:*
> *That as I did freely part*
> *With my glorie and desert,*
> *Left all joyes to feel all smart . . . .*

God is about to say that the soul must 'sign over' all its possessions and delights to Him, when the soul, cornered by this master rhetorician, interrupts: "Ah! no more: thou break'st my heart." This outcry, the last line of the poem, is ambiguous. The soul may have been overcome by God's rehearsal of His generosity; given its materialism, however, it is more likely that the soul is resisting the terms about to be imposed. The second interpretation is the one intended by Herbert. He makes this clear by beginning the next poem with a complaint of man's earthliness: "Why do I languish thus, drooping and dull,/ As if I were all earth?" (*Dullnesse*)

## Logical, but not positivist

The available evidence supports the contention that the seventeenth-century reader expected from a poem a delight which is different in kind from that which a modern audience appreciates. Herbert's contemporaries would have rejected out of hand Wordsworth's idea of poetry as originating in a "spontaneous overflow of powerful feeling." Granted, literature for them was rhetoric, and rhetoric served to sway the reader's feelings towards the pursuit of whatever seemed honest and just. Yet the persuasive power of their rhetoric is not the equivalent of what we mean by the 'emotional power' of poetry. We tend to polarize feeling and thinking. Modern readers often heed primarily the emotive and sensuous qualities of poetic language because they have come to feel that the poet offers little else; they expect of him no *true* statement.

Seventeenth-century readers would have been surprised by such an attitude. Their schooling had inculcated in them the beliefs that words express reality and that the quest for the right word is of paramount importance. They knew that speech embodies feeling and attitudes, but they found no conflict between the emotive and sensuous function of a word on the one hand, and its capacity to express an idea on the other. They had not yet polarized thought and feeling. They saw as yet no opposition between literature and science; the poet still was, as he had been for Sidney, "of all sciences . . . the Monarch."

When we read a modern poem, we usually look upon its 'truth' as relative to the poet; he comes up to our critical norm when he gives us a sensuous reaction of his emotional experience of that truth. The contemporaries of Donne, Herbert, and Milton did not think of poetry as self-expression. This followed from their identification of poetry with rhetoric. The poet must persuade; therefore, he did not turn in upon himself, but divided his attention between his subject matter and his audience. His aim was to light up his matter from a perspective that his audience could also adopt. He must communicate, not himself, but his topic. It followed that in his choice of diction he put the emphasis on the conceptual core of the word, that is, on the known meaning(s) that he could share with his audience.

The seventeenth-century poet was inventive in the manipulation of his vocabulary, but his inventiveness did not imply the idea of 'original discovery.' In the textbooks of logic the *topics* of 'invention' were the means by which one might gather all the available information on a thing, subject, or person. Having collected his materials, the writer moved on to 'judgment': their combination into a persuasive argument. We may say that the poet approached words in a similar fashion: He 'invented' the known uses of a word and made a judgment about the aptness of fusing some or all of these senses. The result of this approach to words is the multiplicity of meanings already demonstrated in Donne and Herbert.

If modern readers tend to look upon this as mere punning, Herbert's controlled development of various meanings throughout a poem may convince them that his word-play is more than a trick of style. We should also remember that, whatever we mean by the phrase 'the poetic imagination,' the phenomenon was not popular in the literary criticism of that period. 'Invention,' 'judgment,' and 'style' divided between them the office of poetry and tested each detail that was to be part of a literary composition. Alexander Pope was unintentionally quite correct when he declared that "Donne had no imagination, but as much wit I think as any writer can possibly have."[5] Even Milton, who gives that imaginative description of the poet "soaring in the high region of his fancies with his garland and singing robes about him,"[6] was in practice a *faber,* a 'maker' or 'artisan.' The style of *Paradise Lost* is impressively grand, yet Milton's diction often follows what is usually thought of as being a distinctly 'metaphysical' practice: frequent play on the derivations and differences of words.

## The grand style in detail

He ceas'd; and *Satan* staid not to reply,                    1010
But glad that now his Sea should find a shore,
With fresh alacritie and force renew'd
Springs upward like a Pyramid of fire
Into the wild expanse, and through the shock
Of fighting Elements, on all sides round                      1015
Environ'd wins his way; harder beset
And more endanger'd, then when *Argo* pass'd
Through *Bosporus* betwixt the justling Rocks,
Or when *Ulysses* on the Larbord shunnd
*Charybdis,* and, by th' other whirlpool steard.              1020
So he with difficulty and labour hard
Mov'd on, with difficulty and labour hee;
But hee once past, soon after when man fell,
Strange alteration! Sin and Death amain
Following his track, such was the will of Heav'n,             1025
Pav'd after him a broad and beat'n way
Over the dark Abyss, whose boiling Gulf
Tamely endur'd a Bridge of wondrous length
From Hell continu'd reaching th' utmost Orb
Of this frail World; by which the Spirits perverse            1030
With easy intercourse pass to and fro
To tempt or punish mortals, except whom
God and good Angels guard by special grace.
But now at last the sacred influence
Of light appears, and from the walls of Heav'n                1035
Shoots far into the bosom of dim Night
A glimmering dawn; here Nature first begins
Her fardest verge, and *Chaos* to retire
As from her outmost works a brok'n foe
With tumult less and with less hostile din,                   1040
That *Satan* with less toil, and now with ease
Wafts on the calmer wave by dubious light
And like a weather-beaten Vessel holds
Gladly the Port, though Shrouds and Tackle torn;
Or in the emptier waste, resembling Air,                      1045
Weighs his spread wings, at leasure to behold
Farr off th' Empyreal Heav'n, extended wide
In circuit, undetermind square or round,
With Opal Towrs and Battlements adorn'd
Of living Saphire, once his native Seat;                      1050

And fast by hanging in a golden Chain
This pendant world, in bigness as a Starr
Of smallest Magnitude close by the Moon.
Thither full fraught with mischievous revenge,
Accurst, and in a cursed hour, he hies.                    1055
*Paradise Lost*, II,

Some aspects of Milton's style in this description immediately catch the ear. The expansive swell of the lines is partly achieved by the frequent presentation of subjects and actions in pairs—to mention a few: "with fresh alacritie *and* force renew'd," "Sin *and* Death," "tempt *or* punish," "God *and* good Angels," "Nature . . . *and Chaos;*" light "appears . . . *and* shoots," Satan "holds the port . . . *Or* . . . weighs his spread wings." Milton's pleasure in balance and antithesis is especially conspicuous in the extended simile that compares Satan's treacherous voyage to the dangerous courses of ancient heroes. Satan is "harder beset/ *And* more endanger'd"; the comparison is split into two parts: "then when *Argo* . . . *Or* when *Ulysses.*" The reference to Ulysses is again subdivided: "on the Larbord . . . *and* by th' other whirlpool . . ." (1016–1020).

Milton also dilates his descriptive style by using long, compound sentences that are very plainly structured. The order of the first sentence, which covers seven lines, is a string of casually connected main verbs: "He ceas'd; *and* Satan staid not . . . *But* . . . Springs upward . . . *and* . . . wins his way . . . ." Milton prefers the common co-ordinating conjunction so much that even the three parts that make up his description of Satan's trip are linked by a casual "But." The first part shows us Satan's take-off and informs us of the extreme difficulty of his undertaking. Then suddenly the poet leaves him to talk of the events subsequent to the devil's successful seduction of mankind: "*But* hee once past, soon after when men fell . . . ." Only after the completion of the poet's exposé do we return to Satan's interrupted voyage and view with him the prospect of heaven and the pendant world. Here again the transition is apparently careless: "*But* now at last the sacred influence/ Of light appears . . . ."

The copiousness of Milton's rhetoric and his predilection for co-ordinating sentences, and even paragraphs, compel the reader forward. This propulsion is enhanced by the constant use of alliteration and assonance, linking the lines into units of sound.

The sibilants of the opening verses are one example of this; another is the repeated *i* in lines 1013–1016: "like . . . fire . . . wild . . . fighting . . . sides . . . Environ'd." The feeling of restless movement is further increased by the frequent enjambements and Milton's occasional reversal of the normal adjective-noun order; such combinations as "force renew'd," "Spirits perverse," and "tumult less" lengthen the line by giving the adjective a stress equal to that of the noun.

The net effect of the stylistic devices so far discussed is a forward momentum that is rhythmical, melodious, but also counterlogical; it does not invite us to think, it merely urges us on. Yet we know that Milton wants us to think about the significance of the events recorded in *Paradise Lost:* He breaks off the stirring description of Satan's grand effort with a discourse on its effect on mankind. He clearly means to deflate our excited response to the devil's outward exploits. The poet's interruption is meant as a warning not to be led astray by these seeming heroics, and focuses our attention on their evil portent. Only after this correction of our perspective are we allowed another look at Satan's enterprise. And if we look closely enough at the details in Milton's style, we see that the oracular, incantatory, and counterlogical quality of Milton's verse is only part of its effect. In fact, the style of *Paradise Lost* joins two contending forces: One is its counterlogical momentum; the other, a strict emphasis on the meaning of the events that are so expansively rendered.

There are a number of ways in which Milton directs the reader to pay careful attention to his words. Although the co-ordinating conjunctions of the first paragraph make us read on, Milton tucks a great deal of commentary into his sentences by means of qualifying phrases, appositions, and participial constructions. The very absence of *sub*-ordinating conjunctions demands that we ourselves supply the relationship of these parenthetical phrases to the main verbs; they must be meaningfully set off in the reading, and this demands that we keep modulating our voice in order to render them intelligible.

For a right reading of *Paradise Lost* we had best know the etymology of its Latinate diction, for Milton often asks us to take derivations into account. Sometimes he himself supplies the meaning: "on all sides round" (1015) translates 'Environ'd'; "hanging"

(1052) is a variant for "pendant" in the next line. But when the fallen angels are called "Spirits perverse" (1030), Milton implies more than their wickedness: "perverse" (from *per-vertere*, 'to make a complete turn') means that they are physically turned around; from hell, their proper abode, they ascend to earth. Their effect on man is also literally perverse: They turn him away from heaven and towards hell. Their "intercourse" (1031) is not merely 'contact' but an actual *cursus inter*, a 'causeway' between two points. By the "influence of light" (1034) Milton has in mind more than 'vague effect,' for influence really means 'a flowing in'; the movement of the sacred light is stressed in "shoots into" and "glimmering" (1035–36). In line 1040 ("With tumult less and with less hostile din") "tumult" is, at first glance, a mere synonym of "din." Yet the Latin *tumultus* also means 'swell,' particularly the swelling of a wave. Satan's trip has throughout been compared to a voyage across the sea ("glad that now his Sea should find a shore"); his dangers were greater than those of Jason and Ulysses; he traversed a "boiling Gulf." Milton's "tumult" continues the imagery of Satan as mariner: Now the *swell* of the ocean is less, so that Satan "Wafts on the calmer wave" (1042).

What we call the Miltonic *vague*, the indefinite outline of the descriptions in *Paradise Lost*, is often achieved by etymological word-play. The view of heaven as "undetermind square or round" (1048) is, in this passage, only one of several instances in which the poet emphasizes that his language is incapable of expressing his vision. His vision is true, but his pictorial representation is always a partially false approximation. Therefore, the use of "undetermind" is a flat denial of the poet's description of heaven. For the same reason, in lines 1026–1027 the roadway built by Sin and Death crosses a "därk Abyss" that is also a "boiling Gulf." A gulf has a bottom, somewhere, but *abyssos* means bottomless; the result of Milton's combination amounts to saying that Chaos is neither one nor the other, or both at the same time: At any rate, it is indescribable. An ironic instance of Milton's undercutting his own magnificent descriptions occurs in lines 1043–1046. All along, in our mind's eye, we have been thinking of Satan as flying, winging his way through Chaos. The many references to him as a seafarer were, we thought, part of an extended simile: Satan's flight to the Universe is like a voyage of discovery across the ocean. Now, at the end of Milton's description, we are told that Satan

> Wafts on the calmer wave by dubious light
> And like a weather-beaten Vessel holds
> Gladly the Port, though Shrouds and Tackle torn . . . .
>
>                                      1042–44

We are still under the impression that the image of the ship is a simile for the devil's real flight. But Milton adds

> Or in the emptier waste, resembling Air,
> Weighs his spread wings . . . .

The word that gives it all away is *or*. As far as the poet is concerned, we may choose to look upon Satan as a mariner, *or* we may regard him as a more successful Icarus. It makes no real difference, for the conventional representation of angels as winged creatures is no less an image than the poet's analogy of Satan to a ship's captain. The poet's descriptions are pictures for the human eye; his inexpressible vision lies somewhere between or behind their shifting combinations, somewhere beyond the edge of sight.

Evidently, Milton, even when "soaring in the high regions of his fancy," was busily 'inventing' and 'judging' the fitness of his vocabulary. He often teases our capacity for attention by the repetition of a word. When Satan, in Book IV, approaches paradise, that happy place appears as "a woodie Theatre/ Of stateliest view" (141–142). "Theater," from the Greek Θεᾶσθαι (to behold), is 'a place for viewing.' Accordingly, the wall of paradise gives Adam a "prospect large/ Into his neather Empire, neighbouring round." A little later, we meet the word 'prospect' again. As Satan alights on the Tree of Life and sits there "devising Death," he "only us'd/ For prospect, what well us'd had bin the pledge/ Of immortality" (199–200). The repetition of the word makes us think about a possible similarity between Satan and Adam. They both use their vantage points as a lookout. Yet *pro-spicere* also means 'to look forward to'; Satan sees into the future, anticipating the death of man, while Adam, unwittingly, looks from the walls of paradise into his own future: the perplexing jungle below that will be his only abode after the Fall.

Coming nearer to paradise, Satan enters a balmy atmosphere

that can "drive/ All sadness but despair" (155–156), and the meaning of that last word is repeated in Milton's comparison of the devil "to them who sail/ Beyond the *Cape of Hope.*" Milton reminds us here of Satan's limitation; the devil's ascent from hell notwithstanding, he is beyond the point of no return in his quest for grandeur. He only *looks* impressive. Even though paradise is protected by "Insuperable highth of loftiest shade" (138), he enters with an easy, athletic grace: "At one slight bound high overleap'd all bound" (181). The first "bound" means 'leap,' the second 'boundary.' Physical frontiers evidently mean nothing to a fallen angel. However, "all bound" does not imply that the devil can transgress the moral limitations imposed on him by God. He remains a spirit in bondage—Milton has reminded us of that some lines earlier, in the comparison of Satan to Asmodeus, whom God punished for murder by driving him "to Egypt, there fast bound" (171). Satan too is a murderer, and in spite of his restless activity he is still "fast bound" in his own land of bondage, hell.

Milton announces his intention to play upon the "derivations and differences" of words in the first lines of his epic when he supplies the literal translation of "mortal tast" in the phrase "Brought Death into the World." Even the fallen angels know how to use this language of simultaneous translation: God's "Sole reigning" is called the *"Tyranny* of Heav'n" (I, 129); "our Glory extinct" becomes our "happy state . . . swallow'd up" (I, 141–142); "uncreated" is "Devoid of sense and motion" (II, 150–151); they use such Anglo-Latin combinations as "sustain and bear" (II, 209) and "Useful of hurtful, prosperous of adverse" (II, 259).

The use of Latinate diction is wittier, or was for Milton's contemporaries, when the translation is not supplied. Satan, for example, finds, in Book IX, an "unsuspected way" into paradise (69). No one suspects him because no one happens 'to look under' (the literal meaning of *sub-spicere*) the earth, into which Satan disappears. He emerges again "involv'd" in the mist of a fountain (75); "involv'd" from *volvere,* 'to turn,' continues the image of Satan's movement as a vicious circle. He has been circling restlessly around the earth; now he spirals up with the water of the fountain; then he revolves his thoughts ("irresolute/ Of thoughts revolv'd," 87–88) and finally chooses the circling shape of the serpent to embody him.

Milton may have been no practitioner of metaphysical conceits, but it is clear that he was nevertheless fond of linguistic intricacies. It is significant, surely, that one of the most critical arguments in *Paradise Lost* finally turns upon an etymological pun. In Book IX, as Eve wishes to exchange her husband's company for solitude, Adam warns her of the danger lurking about. When she accuses him of doubting her "firm Faith and Love" (286), he attempts first to placate her by saying that he merely wishes to protect her from having to suffer someone's unpleasant advances. He then adds, however, that she must not underestimate an enemy who could prevail over angels. It is therefore better that husband and wife remain together for their mutual support. Eve retorts: "How are we happie, still in fear of harm?" (326) Did not God plan this garden as a perfect abode for man? According to her, Adam's argument implies that paradise affords no security, and she dismisses his view:

> "Let us not then suspect our happie State
> Left so imperfect by the Maker wise,
> As not secure to single and combin'd."
>                                 337–339

Adam's answer distinguishes between different meanings of 'secure.' The word, etymologically, is a combination of *se* and *cura.* The latter is 'care,' but the seventeenth century was less sure of the meaning and derivation of *se.* According to Ryder's *Latine Dictionarie* (1640) it was sometimes a contraction of *semus* ('imperfect'), or *secus* ('according to'), or *sine* ('without'); *se* is also a form of the reflexive pronoun 'oneself' or 'himself.' Eve's "secure" obviously means *sine cura*, 'free from care.' Adam admits that the word, so interpreted, indeed applies to their condition in paradise; God has created them free from external danger:

> "O Woman, best are all things as the will
> Of God ordain'd them, his creating hand
> Nothing imperfect or deficient left
> Of all that he Created, much less Man,
> Or aught that might his happie State secure,
> Secure from outward force . . . ."
>                                 343–348

The repetition of "secure"—once as verb, then as adjective—

emphasizes its importance in the argument; for after Adam has qualified its use in the sense of *sine cura,* he goes on to say that it also implies that man must 'care for himself.' In fact, the two senses are interdependent: man in paradise is 'secure' or 'free from fear of external harm,' *because* he is 'secure' or 'in his own care.' Adam continues:

> ". . . within himself
> The danger lies, yet lies within his power;
> Against his will he can receive no harm."

Milton's use of word-play at this significant juncture in his epic would appeal to his contemporaries. Adam tries to convey the truth, and he must move Eve to accept it with all the logical and rhetorical skills at his disposal. To a modern audience, Adam might seem to be wrangling, but to Milton's early readers, Adam's argument would constitute evidence of his superiority over Eve; his greater linguistic skill was proof of his better mind. It was also proof of Milton's stature as poet. The 'organ voice,' his grand style, aimed at swaying the audience, but Milton knew that rhetoric mediates between the emotions and the reason. He desired the reader's assent rather than submission. Hence, the word-play in *Paradise Lost* was intended to keep the reader's mind ever vigilant as he follows the poet's quick intelligence and lively insight.[7]

# Chapter Four

## ❧

# Religion and Literature

## The strife of confutation

The reverence now accorded to the sciences was in the early seventeenth century given to the instruction in the ways of God, the desired polity of His Church, and the order of worship most agreeable to Him. The fear of God being, according to the psalmist, the beginning of wisdom, the child's religious training began early, informally at its mother's knee, but formally at petty school. All that Anthony à Wood remembers from his attendance there, he sums up briefly: "in 1637, he was put to schoole to learne to read the psalter." [1]

At grammar school the day usually began and ended with a reading of a chapter of the English Bible, followed by a psalm, a pious exhortation, and a hymn. These twice-daily exercises were not purely devotional. The scholars of the lower grammar school followed the Bible lesson in an English text, but those in upper grammar school used a Latin or Greek version. The students were encouraged to ask each other questions pertinent to the chapter or passage that had been read. Their authority in this miniature inquisition was Eusebius Paget's *History of the Bible, briefly collected, by way of question and answer* (1613).

Hoole advises that students in the upper forms always carry with them a copy of Matthias Martinius' *Memoriale Biblicum* (1603), "by which they may put in mind at all times, what passages they may finde in any chapter." Accurate knowledge of Holy Scripture was, of course, advantageous in argument; one could always score a point against one's opponent with an appropriate quotation

from the word of God. The frequent, almost ubiquitous, inter-
spersion of biblical references in the literature of the age was not
solely intended as an indication of piety; Augustine had urged
that for the wise man "it is above all necessary to remember the
words of Scripture . . . He shall give delight with his proofs."[2]
An opponent would find it difficult to quarrel with the verdict
of God, although he could always, and usually did, debate its
interpretation. God Himself was assumed to be a master of logic
and rhetoric in His communication with man. Many textbooks
in the arts of discourse, especially of the Ramist variety, took their
examples of arguments and figures from the Bible. The minute
division and subdivision of a text, the precise and, to modern
readers, precious analysis of its single words, the building of
conceits on the basis of biblical word order—in brief, the sermon
style of Lancelot Andrewes—was not novel to an educated audience of the age. Naturally, the court preacher far exceeded the
schoolmaster in subtlety and style; Andrewes gave virtuoso performances, but his genre was well known.

"Sundaies the pillars are,/ On which heav'n's palace arched
lies," says Herbert in his meditative poem devoted to that day. For
the grammar school boys Sunday left little leisure for recreation.
According to the Reverend Hoole, the master met with his scholars
an hour before church service and taught them a part of
catechetical doctrine. After reciting a psalm and a prayer, the
students were marched off to church in a body. In the afternoon
they convened again at school, where the master examined them
on what they remembered of the sermon. The little ones had only
to repeat the text of the preacher, or a proof, or some pious
sentence that had struck them. Older boys had to write down the
text, the points of doctrine developed from it, as well as the
"Reason, Uses, Motives, and Directions, with the Quotations of
Scripture-places." The highest form had to reconstruct the entire
sermon. Then the master elaborated upon a memorable point,
and, after another psalm and prayer, might "comfortably dismisse
them to their several homes."

The demand for closely heeding the preacher's word led to the
practice of taking copious notes during the sermon, a habit that
the grammar school student often continued after his matriculation at one of the universities. Sir Simonds d'Ewes writes in his

diary that at Cambridge in 1618, "I continued, like-wise, my former course of noting sermons." [3] The few women who pretended to intellectual status apparently demonstrated this in public by imitating the men in "noting sermons." Sir Ralph Verney warned: "Let not your daughter learn Latin or shorthand; the difficulty of the first may keep her from that vice, for so I must esteem it in a woman; but the easiness of the other may be a prejudice to her; for the pride of taking sermon notes hath made multitudes of women most unfortunate." [4] It seems that Sir Simonds d'Ewes also used a kind of shorthand as he listened to the preacher, for in the evening he would retire to his rooms to reorganize his notes. He did all this for pleasure and, presumably, spiritual profit. In his day, undergraduates were no longer officially examined on their attentiveness in church. However, during the Commonwealth, sermons were thought so important that, according to Anthony à Wood, the parliamentary visitors required of all undergraduates and bachelors that they rehearse the Sunday sermon to a person of learning and piety.[5]

The efficacy of sermonizing had long been assumed in the academic communities, and the Laudian Code for Oxford only affirmed existing statutes when it stipulated the obligatory attendance at the university sermons, delivered in English every Sunday during the term and in Latin at the opening of the term. In addition, morning sermons were to be given every day in Lent, and afternoon sermons throughout the academic year.[6] The university sermons were supplemented by the doctrinal oratory from the pulpits of the college chapels, and each college had its own means of confirming the students in their faith. Pembroke, for example, demanded full attendance at regular catechetical lectures,[7] and Emmanuel held a weekly disputation in divinity.[8]

Continued religious controversy led to an emphasis on biblical exegesis and to the examination of the early history and fathers of the Church. Thus each party hoped to build around its own religious confession a sort of fortress from which it might safely attack all opponents. The English kept themselves informed of the theological and biblical scholarship of the continental Catholic, Huguenot, Genevan, and Dutch divines. A well-read theologian was inevitably a master in the art of explication. The Reverend Anthony Burgess composed *145 Expository Sermons on the whole 17th Chapter according to John* (1656). That chapter consists of twenty-six verses, so that Burgess had to take second place to the Reverend Arthur Hildeshan, who had, in 1635, published 152 sermons on a mere nineteen verses of the Fifty-first Psalm. For poorer scholars, William Crow paved a pathway to heavenly riches in his systematic arrangement of the English commentaries on Scripture: *An exact Collection or Catalogue of our English writers on the Old and New Testament* (1663), an index of references to comments on each book of the Bible, on each chapter, and often on nearly every verse. In addition, the exegete could turn to important continental sources available in translation: the *Douay Commentary* (1609), Giovanni Diodati's *Pious Annotations* (1643), and the *Dutch Annotations* (1657). The layman could pick and choose from an array of expositions of the Creed, the Lord's Prayer, and the Commandments, or he could find his theology capsuled in numerous "Marrows," "Sums," and "Bodies" of Christian religion. These little books proved even more vendible than had been the popular "courtesy" books for elegant deportment in the previous age.[9]

This theological bent is one of the delayed effects of the Reformation. The notion that the early sixteenth-century protest against Rome and papal supremacy was an assertion of individual freedom is by now an exploded cliché. There was a degree of difference between Renaissance humanism and the motive of the Protestant reformers. The Reformation's stress on the need to save souls skirted the Erasmian defense of intellectual freedom. The early reformers were less dogmatic than Rome because they were more evangelical; they preached the message of the reconciliation of the individual soul to God. To the extent that they sought to cancel out the authority of bishop and priest as mediators of God's grace, their movement might be labelled 'liberal.' Ironically, however, the evangelical bent led to a revival of dogmatism among Protestant sects. On the assumption that the word of God contained the grounds of salvation and marked off the road to heaven, individual reading and study of Scripture was made mandatory. Yet, in deciding the disputes that arose from the varying interpretations of the Divine Word, authority came in again. There followed a proliferation of 'creeds,' 'confessions,' and 'articles of religion,' carefully formulated and authoritatively set forth. Thus the practice of Protestant churches curiously reversed a basic

Reformation principle; in theory, Scripture preceded dogma, but, in practice, dogma came before Scripture. Each church taught its members to read the Bible in the light of the official creed. Not so long after the 'freedom' of the Reformation had been first proclaimed, certain Protestant sects, Calvinism in particular, became as authoritarian as Rome. Usually the Protestant was involved in a war on two fronts: both against the nonbiblical doctrine of Rome and against the Protestants who dissented from his own interpretation of Scripture.

In seventeenth-century England many of the heated disputes involved the question of 'ecclesiastical polity' or Church discipline. Frequently, the middle class—Puritan, Parliamentarian, and antiprelatic—found no satisfaction in the doctrine preached by the vicars and curates duly ordained and installed according to the order of the established Church of England. A wealthy merchant, a town corporation, or a group of parishioners often decided to supplement what they considered their spiritual want by endowing a lectureship. The lecturers invited to accept an appointment according to the terms of the endowment were mostly men trained in divinity but without the advantage and financial security of a benefice in the Church of the realm. The stipend they drew from the lectureships freed them from economic pressure and encouraged them in their resistance to the ecclesiastical hierarchy. Their lectures or sermons reflected not the theological and political views of the court and the archbishop of Canterbury, but those of the increasingly independent middle class. Often the incumbent Anglican priest preached to please king and bishop, while the lecturer preached to please the congregation. Lectures, usually given in the afternoon, grew increasingly popular, and the established Church tried repeatedly either to abolish or control them. Archbishop Laud fought them so vigorously that in 1638 most lectureships were vacant, to be filled again as the tide turned against "prelatical episcopacy" after 1640.[10]

The parishioners of the Reverend Robert Dove of Islington furnish an example of the kind of dissatisfaction that could be caused by the incumbent Anglican priest. They complained in 1640 "that the Communion table was turned altar wise by Mr. Dove and by the parishioners turned around three times, and as often set altar wise again by Mr. Dove or his orders, and that he preacheth that who so puts on his hat in the church, service or no service, he will punish him."[11] Parishioners thus provoked by the papist abominations of their minister were often willing to pay for a lecturer to whom they could listen with or without hat, following their own convictions about pious propriety.

Opposition to the hierarchy gave the dissenting Protestants a common goal until the Westminister Assembly in 1643 recommended the abolition of episcopacy. Thereupon, the former antiprelatical parties wrangled with each other. The Presbyterians wished to impose a strict form of church discipline of their own, whereas the Independents believed that each congregation could well govern itself. The former, says Anthony à Wood, "for the most part, preached nothing but damnation: the other not, but rather for libertie. Yet both joyne together to pluck downe and silence the prelaticall preachers, or at least, expose their way to scorne."[12] Together, Independents and Presbyterians thoroughly cleansed the college chapels at Oxford and Cambridge. The use of organs, candles, incense, surplice, and the old Book of Common Prayer was forbidden. After the Commonwealth, all the 'papist' practices were immediately restored:

> The first matter, therefore, that the restored persons looked after was to put themselves in the most prelaticall garb that could be, and the rather, that they might encourage others, especially those of the intervall, to doe the like; to restore all signes of monarchy in the Universitie, the Common prayer, surplice and certaine customes, as I have partly before told you; to reduce the Universitie to the old way of preaching and praying; to make the intervall way—which was long, tedious, and too practicall (not without puling, whining, and ugly faces)—neglected and ridiculous and especially to be avoided by those young preachers initiated in the Presbyterian and Independent discipline, which they saw enclining much (for hopes of preferment) to the prelaticall.[13]

The return to the surplice occasioned such ire among its opponents at Oxford that in January 1660 a group of them stole the surplices of Christ College and threw them into the common privy. This in turn so enraged the dean and the canons of the church that they publicly threatened that the guilty would have their ears cut off in the market place.

> . . . The Presbyterians were wonderfully pleased at this action, laughed hartily among themselves, and some in my hearing have

protested that if they knew the person that did this heroick act they would convey to him an encouraging gratuity. Soone after came out a ballad or lampoone, made as 'twas reported by one Thomas Smith bachelor of Arts of Christ Church, intituled 'Lowe's Lamentation,' or the lamentation of Edward Lowe organist of Christ Church—the beginning of which was this:—

> 'Have pitty on us all, good Lairds,
> For surely wee are all uncleane. . . .'[14]

Given the intensity and the political consequences of the religious controversies, one did not have to be a zealous divine to show an interest in theological issues. Even so worldly a man as Sir John Suckling, who enjoyed no reputation for the holiness of his life, made his contribution in a treatise called *An Account of Religion by Reason* (1637). The title is in part misleading, for Sir John wrote an orthodox commentary on conventional topics such as the Trinity, Incarnation, Redemption, and Resurrection.

King Charles was too busy building his collection of great works of art to be a theologian, but his father James thought of himself, not without justification, as a learned divine. His two hobbies were hunting and theology, and it is difficult to discern whether he preferred quelling an heretical opponent to shooting a defenseless deer. When Cardinal Bellarmine, the great Roman apologist of the day, denied James's supremacy over the Church of England, the king answered him in an *Apologie for the Oath of Allegiance* (1607). Bellarmine, of course, replied in print. James countered with another pamphlet, *A Premonition to all Christian Monarchies, Free Princes and States* (1609). This still did not silence the cardinal. The king set Lancelot Andrewes to work to continue the debate, which by then had become an international dispute to which dozens of scholars decided to contribute their zeal, wit, learning, and invective.[15]

When it came to matters of religion, James lost all political perspective and managed to alienate many of his friends. He was himself by training a doctrinaire Calvinist. The majority of his enemies in the realm, opposed to James's cherished royal prerogative, were of the same persuasion. The king detested the views of the Arminians, an 'heretical' party that had arisen within the Calvinist fold. He even sent an English deputation to the Synod of Dort (1618) to support Calvinist orthodoxy against the

Arminians. In so doing, James completely ignored political reality: Many of his loyal supporters espoused Arminian views. Arminianism, in fact, was a quiet, but most significant movement for the development of religious thought and attitudes in England.

## Arminius, Great Tew, and Little Gidding

The origin of Arminianism illustrates how much the Reformation sects insisted on the need for absolute certitude and agreement concerning every detail of their creeds and confessions. The Calvinist believed that God had predestined the salvation or damnation of the individual soul, or, as the Lambeth Articles of 1595 put it: "It is not in the will and power of every man to be saved." [16] The question arose, then, whether predestination was a punitive consequence of Adam's Fall or a divine disposition antecedent to the creation of the world. Those who held the first view were called Infralapsarians, the others Supralapsarians. In other words, the Infralapsarians believed that it was within the power of Adam to save himself, but because he sinned, his offspring is without that power; the Supralapsarians held that even Adam had not the freedom to choose for or against God: His Fall was part of the divine, predestined pattern.

A Dutch theologian, Jacobus Arminius (1560–1609), had been asked to undertake the defense of the Supralapsarian point of view. Yet, as he examined the doctrine he was supposed to champion, he concluded that it was false. Not only that, he began to question the other tenets laid down by Calvin and the latter's disciple Beza. Upon the appointment of Arminius as professor of divinity at Leyden, his heretical views became a public issue, and the controversy about them spread from Holland to England. Arminianism was formally repudiated by the Calvinist Synod of Dort in 1618. The edict of the synod forced the Arminians to become a separate sect, also called the party of the Remonstrants.

The main tenets of Arminianism varied significantly from Calvinist orthodoxy. The Arminian did not differ from the Calvinist in granting supreme authority to Scripture. Yet Calvinism held that the word of Scripture had power over man's reason and conscience and could be used by the Church against heretics. For the Arminians, however, the authority of the Bible lay in the beauty and effectiveness of that document; the truth of Scripture would inevitably reveal itself to the well-inclined reader. Therefore, the Arminians would not force anyone who was not in reason and conscience convinced of a certain truth to accept that truth on biblical grounds only. The just man, they said, might approach the Bible freely and would eventually recognize its truth without having his reason and conscience bound by ecclesiastical rule; he would hear the voice of God in his reading. Arminianism accepted, in principle, the freedom of private interpretation, the liberty of 'prophesying.'

The second Arminian tenet follows from the first: 'Confessions,' 'creeds,' and 'articles' are not declarations of what must be believed, but historical documents showing what their authors believed. They reflect different expressions of faith in different ages. The Arminians made no exception for their own *Remonstrants' Confession*. It was meant as a guide, not as a tribunal regulating the intercourse of man with God.

Finally, Arminianism distinguished between essential and subsidiary points of doctrine. For the essential points of doctrine they urged the study of the Bible, the Apostles' Creed, and the writings of the early Church. They hoped that in these documents all Protestant sects might find some areas of agreement that would reduce the divisiveness and strife between them. Subsidiary doctrine was for the Arminians a matter of private devotion and conduct.[17]

Arminianism soon gained ground in England. Milton's faith is based on Remonstrant principles, and Arminian arguments form the structure of Jeremy Taylor's *Liberty of Prophesying* (1647). For a time, the center of Arminian study was Great Tew, the seat of Lucius Cary (1610–1643), Second Lord Falkland. His father had been lord deputy of Ireland, and Lucius Cary studied at Trinity College, Dublin, to which many Calvinist professors from Cambridge had repaired in the later years of Elizabeth's reign, in fear of her vengeance against the rising tide of Puritan discontent. The Second Lord Falkland seemed to have been dissatisfied with the rigidity of his teachers. On his return to England, young Lucius befriended Ben Jonson and such other literary lights as Suckling, Davenant, Sandys, Carew, and Waller. He also established a theological salon at Great Tew. Frequent guests were

Gilbert Sheldon, later archbishop of Canterbury, George Morley, the future bishop of Winchester, and John Earle, the author of the famous collection of 'characters' entitled *Microcosmography* (1628) and later bishop of Salisbury. The finest minds of the circle were John Hales and William Chillingworth. The first, the "ever-memorable Mr. John Hales of Eton,"[18] had been an observer at the Synod of Dort and has left a series of letters describing its proceedings. The bitter contentiousness of the synod seems to have offended his irenic disposition. He, Falkland, and Chillingworth were the leading English proponents of a rational theology based on Arminian principles. All three wrote on the subject, but their views are most eloquently summed up in Chillingworth's *The Religion of Protestants a Safe Way to Salvation* (1637). The following passage shows the religious latitude advocated by the men of Great Tew:

> . . . If men would allow that the way to heaven is not narrower now than Christ left it, His yoke no heavier than He made it; that the belief of no more difficulties is required now to salvation than was in the primitive Church; that no error is in itself destructive and exclusive from salvation now which was not then; if, instead of being zealous Papists, earnest Calvinists, rigid Lutherans, they would become themselves, and be content that others should be, plain and honest Christians; if all men would believe the Scripture, and, freeing themselves from prejudice and passion, would sincerely endeavor to find the true sense of it, and live according to it, and require no more of others than to do so; nor denying their communion to any that do so, would so order their public service of God that all which do so may, without scruple, or hypocrisy, or protestation against any part of it, join with them in it,—who doth not see that, since all necessary truths are plainly and evidently set down in Scripture, there would of necessity be among all men, in all things necessary, unity of opinion? And, notwithstanding any other differences that are or could be, unity of communion, and charity, and mutual toleration, by which means all schism and heresy would be banished the world, and those wretched contentions which now rend and tear in pieces, not the coat, but the members and bowels of Christ, which mutual pride, and tyranny, and killing, and damning, would fain make immortal, should speedily receive a most blessed catastrophe.[19]

The members of the Great Tew circle attempted to nurture an ecumenical spirit that would put an end to the bitterness of religious strife. An alternate road out of division and dissension was to concentrate not on theology but on the practice of the devout life. That path was followed by the members of Little Gidding, a community of families who had left the care of the world's business to God in order to dedicate themselves to their own spiritual advancement.[20] The founding of Little Gidding by Nicolas Ferrar and a few of his friends is representative of the desire for solitude that is one of the characteristics of the period. The literary record of the age contains many names of men who answered an urge to withdraw from the world. After the loss of his friends and the frustration of his "court hopes," Herbert lived in humble seclusion at Bemerton. Crashaw sought solace in Little Gidding, became an obscure exile in Paris and Rome, and died as a Roman Catholic priest in Loreto. After brief service on the royalist side in the Civil War, Vaughan spent the second half of his long life in obscurity at Newton-by-Usk. Aside from a few details about his background and education, hardly anything is known about Herrick's adult life in the years before, during, and after the Commonwealth; all we know for certain is that he was vicar of Dean Prior in rural Devonshire from 1630 to 1647 and from 1660 to his death in 1674. We know virtually nothing about the life of Thomas Traherne. It may be worth noting that Marvell's greatest outburst of lyrical genius seems to have coincided with his retirement to Nun Appleton House, the estate of his patron, Lord Fairfax.

For all their differences in style and temperament, Herbert, Crashaw, Vaughan, Traherne, Herrick, and Marvell generally avoided the theologically divisive issues. Their religious verse is devotional and asks for a return to the basis of the spiritual life: how to grow agreeable to God by submission to His will and the humble acceptance of His mercy. Their spirituality is as little controversial as that of the late-medieval *Imitation of Christ.*

Whatever may have been the currents of seventeenth-century thought that stimulate the historian of ideas to render a many-colored picture of the age, the reader of its religious literary art can approach it without being teased or irritated by the intricacies of theological disputes. Milton was no mean theologian and had carefully defined opinions on doctrinal issues, but his private views are submerged in *Paradise Lost.* His contemporaries saw in his epic an orthodox explication of the Fall of man and the Redemption by Christ. Milton's doctrinal independence was not a matter for academic debate till after the first publication of *De Doctrina Christiana* in 1825. Milton had no intention of denying himself an audience by offending the religious sensibilities of his readers. Knowing how sensitive his readers could be on issues of dogma, he avoided the precise articulation of his theology. His commentary on the loss of paradise follows a broad and traditional interpretation. He wanted to justify the ways of God to man, not to men whose opinions were identical with his own. *Paradise Lost* is essentially latitudinarian: The poet casts his net wide. What is true of the religious epic is true also of the religious lyric. Herbert was demonstrably an Anglican of the *via media,* but the distinctions between his theology and that of others rarely concern him as a poet. *The Temple* is a manual that might teach any Christian to grow in the grace and favor of God. This is what endeared Herbert to so many minds who differed with him on points of doctrine, such as the Roman Catholic Crashaw and the allegedly Puritan Marvell.

## Of paradoxes and problems

The religious literary art of the seventeenth century is not systematized thought. It was composed by thinking men, familiar with a body of reflection—on the nature of man, on life and death, on earth and heaven—which they had inherited as their cultural patrimony. As they composed their works, they made a selection from that heritage and gave it artistic expression. That is why, in deliberating about their philosophical and theological commitments, we should proceed with care; like other legacies, a cultural legacy often contains a good deal of bric-à-brac that the antiquarian finds it hard to identify. It may well be that we can draw a chart, showing a linear progression from an age of faith to one of reason, in which the seventeenth century is the period of transition. Yet, even if the human mind moved in such a direction, it does not follow that the literary men of the seventeenth century labored to promote that movement. If we allocate to Sir Thomas Browne, for instance, a place under some such 'ism' as fideism, or scepticism, or rationalism, we are assuming that he was persuaded or pervaded by some powerful contemporary current and betrayed the faith of his fathers to a variety of non-orthodox, 'modern' attitudes. But when Sir Thomas says, in the first paragraph of the *Religio Medici*, that he embraces Christianity because he is obliged thereto "by the principles of grace, and the law of mine owne reason," there is no need to posit that he must inevitably be caught on the horns of *our* dilemma, that of grace or faith *versus* reason. It is unlikely that grace would prompt him to do one thing and reason to do another. Browne's definition of reason was not our modern one. The enlightenment left us with the view of reason as the principle of individual autonomy; for Browne, reason was *recta ratio*, first implanted by God in Adam, and still present, albeit less lustrous, in fallen man. Dimmed by the Fall, reason needs to be complemented by faith, and Browne considered it the mark of a wise man to walk in their combined light.

The frequent paradoxes in seventeenth-century religious expression do not necessarily prove any intellectual discomfort on the part of the writers who managed to invent these clever combinations of irreconcilable opposites. In a systematic treatment of theology an author such as Aquinas may dispose his matter so as to submerge, or even explain away, the contrasts inherent in his belief, but the devotional, affective expression of Christian faith has traditionally used the paradox, for the very reason that Christianity is inevitably paradoxical.

There is, first of all, the paradoxical estimation of the value of human reason. When the Apostle Paul was among the Athenians, he chose to preach at the altar of the Unknown God,[21] but in the Epistle to the Romans he declared that God makes himself known to all men and that worshippers of idols are individually responsible for this profanation.[22] And yet there is no inconsistency in Paul; Christian doctrine admits two kinds of revelation: God's revelation in nature and His revelation in Scripture. God is first known to all men through His manifestation in the visible world—nature is the book of God, and "the heavens," says the psalmist, "declare the glory of God." Thus the pagan arrives at knowledge of God's existence. At the same time, however, the pagan remains unaware of the nature of God: only

Scripture reveals *who* God is. Hence God is simultaneously known and unknown.

Paul's paradox of a known-unknown God points to two different conceptions of truth that Christianity has combined, one Hebraic, the other Hellenic. The Hebraic symbol for truth is the rock—truth depends on the solidity of the authority by which we know something.[23] The Greek conception of truth requires the evidence of something known—its symbol is light. God's revelation in Scripture is the rock of faith; His revelation in nature is the light of faith. Augustine was the first to understand clearly the difference between these two conceptions of truth; it lies behind his distinction between *scientia* and *sapientia:* "The action by which we make good use of temporal things differs from the contemplation of eternal things and the former is classed as knowledge, the latter as wisdom."[24] *Scientia* moves outward and is concerned with the temporal and rational; *sapientia* moves inward and is directed towards the understanding of the eternal. One must keep in mind Augustine's awareness of the difference between Greek knowledge and Christian wisdom if one is to understand his emphasis on faith: "believe that thou mayest understand."[25] For Augustine, classical reason had no starting point except itself; it saw itself as a self-sufficient principle of intelligibility. The philosophical quest of antiquity was motivated by a desire for, and a belief in, the attainment of perfect intelligibility of things both sublunary and transcendental. Augustine believed that no perfect intelligibility exists except in God and that man may approach it only in the measure that he attaches himself to God. The method of attaining intelligibility is therefore from faith to understanding, from the rock to the light: "We are guided in a twofold way, by authority and by reason. In time, authority has the prior place; in matter, reason. . . . Thus it follows that to those desiring to learn the great and hidden good it is authority which opens the door. And whoever enters by it . . . will at length learn how pre-eminently possessed of reason those things are which he pursued before he saw their reason."[26] Faith, then, does not replace reason—the goal remains vision and clarity. Augustine stated clearly the paradox that there is in man's nature "nothing better than the mind and reason" for man's approach towards God, but that, at the same time, mind and reason are insufficient

for the attainment of perfect knowledge of God. It is funda-
mentally Christian to believe that not all things are part of *scientia,*
that metaphysics is not physics, and that in the former man needs
a different kind of measurement. Through study in the book of
nature, reason may attain an awareness of God's existence. However, having established His divinity, reason has reached the limit
of its capacity. Divinity itself is beyond the sphere of the intellect
of man. Having said that God exists, man must declare Him
unknown. Thus metaphysics both affirms and denies—it reaches
finally a mystery that it can only metaphorically describe. At this
point, God comes to man's assistance through Scripture: Only God
can say what He is and describe His *modus operandi,* His action
in time and His direction of history. It is therefore not 'unreasona-
ble' to say that reason may be an obstacle to faith—it is important
for man to know when to surrender his reason. The God of faith
is not the God of philosophers: The latter is a metaphysical
principle, the former a divine agent. Faith is beyond philosophy
in content and in manner: Its content is the revelation of mystery,
its manner is the word of God.

The paradox of reason thus entails the paradox of the place
occupied by man in the totality of the universe. Man's being has
its origin elsewhere, and yet man is not a mere extension of that
Other, First Being; arising from God, man is other than God. If
God is the fullness of being, nothing can exist outside Him. Man,
therefore, exists in Him but, in the phrase of Sir Thomas Browne,
"at a distance." Hence we encounter in the devotional literature
of the seventeenth century the search for oneness and, simultaneously, the recurring complaint of a feeling of loss and separation.

Man is also simultaneously great and small, sacred and profane.
He is created by God and allocated a place in the center of the
universe of God's concern. Herbert's *Man* is a paean on this
pre-eminent position:

> My God, I heard this day,
> That none doth build a stately habitation,
> But he that means to dwell therein.
> What house more stately hath there been,
> Or can be, then is Man? to whose creation
> All things are in decay.

The poem celebrates man's place in God's order: "Man is all symmetrie,/ Full of proportions, one limbe to another." Yet Vaughan, a careful student of Herbert's *Temple,* answers his predecessor's praise in a contrasting poem with the same title. Vaughan's "Man" compares human nature with the order of the universe and finds that man is a weak, discordant creature.

> Man hath stil either toyes, or Care,
> He hath no root, nor to one place is ty'd,
> But ever restless and Irregular
>     About this Earth doth run and ride,
> He knows he hath a home, but scarce knows where,
>         He sayes it is so far
> That he hath quite forgot how to go there.

Both poems are doctrinally correct: Herbert describes man in the state of grace, obedient to God, and therefore the object of divine care; Vaughan emphasizes the sinfulness of human nature, the consequence of the Fall that put man outside God's intended order. It would be false to deduce from the difference between the poems a difference in mood and conviction on the part of their makers. When Vaughan read Herbert's *Man* on man's sacred place, he was reminded of the other, equally traditional view of man's profane inclinations, and wrote his poem as a deliberate contrast.

If the Christian estimation of man's place in the universe is dualistic, the view of the composition of his body and soul is no less so. However, we ought to avoid confusing the Christian distinction between body and soul with the neo-Platonic view, which opposes soul to body. The neo-Platonist holds that the body imprisons the soul, and he emphasizes the strife between these two parts of man. Augustine again defines the orthodox view: "the life of the soul is not one thing, and that of the body another: but both are one and the same, i.e., the life of man as man."[27] The Christian contrast is not between a carnal body and a spiritual soul, but between a man who is carnal in soul and in body, and a man spiritual in soul and body.

The paradoxes and the dualism inherent in Christian belief make it difficult to define the religious positions of seventeenth-century writers. It is no impeachment of orthodoxy to say of one author that he is a mystic, or of another that he follows nature:

Mysticism is theology become luminous, and nature is the rule of God. Nor does it argue a 'dissociation of sensibility' that writers of the period should surrender reason to redeem faith: It is one of the inevitable Christian compromises. The Christian in search of God's favor can always follow the recommendation of Epictetus: "Everything has two handles,—if the one prove hot and not to be touched, we may take the other that is more temperate." To conclude, the search for 'isms' in the early seventeenth century is a difficult and, at any rate, nonliterary preoccupation. What we need for experiencing the impact of the devotional literature of the period is an awareness of certain areas of knowledge that audience and author agreed upon: the received tradition of biblical interpretation and the usual definitions of such terms as Law and Gospel, Nature and Grace, Faith and Works. The catechetical doctrine taught in the schools was the point of take-off for theological dispute as well as for devotional writing. The dissenter might argue against all or part of that doctrine; Donne, Herbert, Vaughan, or Milton elaborated on it for the edification of their readers. All parties, however, assumed that the audience knew the received tenets of belief. For that reason, the next chapter will examine a simple catechism of the age.

# Chapter Five

ॐ

# Nowell's Catechism

## Its author

The only catechism that enjoyed the synodal blessing of the
Church of England until 1643 was written by the Reverend
Alexander Nowell, who lived for nearly a century (1507–1602)
and who was during all his adult years a loyal Anglican.[1] A fellow
of Brasenose College, Oxford, he was appointed master of
Westminister School in 1543, and prebendary of Westminister in
1551. During Mary Tudor's reign he lived in exile, first at
Strasbourg and then at Frankfurt. Upon the accession of Elizabeth
he was well-rewarded for the constancy of his faith. He received
in 1560 a number of simultaneous benefices: the archdeaconry
of Middlesex, the rectory of Saltwood, a stall in Canterbury and
another in St. Peter's Westminster, and the deanery of St. Paul's.
In 1595 he was elected president of his former college, Brasenose.
He occasionally engaged in the constant pamphlet war, always
as a champion of the supremacy of Christian princes in the
ecclesiastical affairs of their realm. He was one of the divines who
tried unsuccessfully to get Edmund Campion, the Jesuit martyr,
to recant.[2]

Nowell's most important contribution to the Reformation in
England was his *Catechism*. In 1562 the Convocation of Bishops
and Clergy advised that "there should be one perfect Catechism
for the bringing up of the youth in godliness, in the schools of
the whole realm."[3] Nowell, then dean of St. Paul's, had already
been composing such a work and submitted it to the convocation,
where it met with immediate approval. It was forwarded to Sir
William Cecil, the queen's principal secretary, who kept it for more

than a year and finally returned it with "certen notes of some lerned man uppon it." Nowell, probably fearful that the "lerned notes" were prompted by the queen, declares in a letter to Cecil that "I . . . altered manie places in it, accordinge to the notes which your honour delyvered unto me, as your honour shall wel perceyve, had you leysure to compare the saide notes (which I have sent agaeine to your honour, even the verie copie it selfe which your honour delyvered me)." [4] The approval of the bishops, granted in 1562, was patently insufficient for Dean Nowell. Not until eight years later, when he was protected by Cecil's approval, did he publish his *Catechismus, sive prima Institutio, Disciplinaque Pietatis Christianae, Latine explicata.* Later in the same year an English translation by Thomas Norton appeared. Between 1570 and 1647 Nowell's *Catechism* went through forty-four editions, in Latin, English, Greek, and all bilingual combinations of these tongues. The Presbyterians replaced it with the *Assembly's Catechism* of 1648, but after the Restoration Nowell's doctrine was still in demand; his work was reissued in 1670, 1673, and 1687. [5] On the testimony of such well-known schoolmasters as Richard Mulcaster, John Brinsley, and Charles Hoole, Nowell's *Catechism* was the standard text for the religious instruction of the young in the late Tudor and early Stuart periods.

Dean Nowell, like so many of his contemporaries, believed that the maintenance of sound Protestant faith required solid education. He endowed a free grammar school at Middleton in Lancashire and a fund for scholarships in Brasenose College. He was a former schoolmaster, and some of his views on pedagogy and education are evident in his *Catechism.* He himself never translated it into the vernacular. The preface to the first edition declares that the work is meant to teach proper Latin, as well as right doctrine, and that the author took great pains to deliver God's truth in the most elegant Ciceronian style. Cicero is also the only secular author to whom Nowell occasionally refers in support of Christian truth; all other references in the margins are to appropriate texts from Scripture. Apparently realizing that the intricate Latinity of his *Catechism* would be an obstacle to pupils who had not yet arrived at an easy comprehension of Ciceronian periods, Nowell adjusted his Latin in his 1571 abridgment of the original and in a further condensation published in 1572. The three versions were popularly refered to as the Little, Middle, and Large Catechism, and students scaled from one to another during their grammar school years.

The method of instruction is the one conjured up by the very word 'catechism': The master proposes a question to which the student supplies a memorized answer. To develop the pupil's retentive capacity, the master frequently recapitulates the doctrine already set forth, showing how "the very orderly course of those matters that we have treated of hath as it were brought us by the hand." Keeping to an orderly course also requires the student to define and divide issues correctly. At the beginning of the detailed explanation of the Creed, for example, the definition of belief is "a true and lively faith," which is distinguished from a "general faith" and from a "dead faith." All three kinds have in common the acceptance of God's word as true, but the general faith gives no prompting to seek God's grace, and the dead faith refuses to believe in God's merciful goodness (Marlowe's Dr. Faustus is an example of a dead believer); only the true and lively faith grants assurance of God's favor and inclines the Christian to the practice of holy life.

As in the study of his classical authors, the pupil must learn to make use of logical arguments. The intellectual agility demanded of him is apparent in the treatment of the Lord's Prayer. After the student has divided that prayer into six petitions, the first three pertaining to the glory of God and the remainder to man's advantage, the Master asks: "Dost thou so sever and divide our profit from God's glory, that thou also makest equal petition between them?" The student replies:

> I do not sever things conjoined, but for plainness of the whole declaration I distinguish things to be severally discerned, for understanding where unto each thing belongeth. Otherwise those things that do properly belong to the glory of God, do also bring most great profit to us; and likewise those things that serve our profit, are all referred to the glory of God. For this ought to be the end whereunto all things must be applied; this ought to be our mark, that God's glory be most amply enlarged. Yet in the meantime, I think that this division in parts shall not be inconvenient, and is made not without reason, but according to the property of the things themselves: because, while we ask those

things that belong properly to the advancing of God's glory, we must for that time omit our own profits, when yet in the later petitions we may well intend our own commodities.

If the reply strikes us as unnecessarily verbose, the student knew that he was making a distinction between two kinds of final causes. The first is the cause of all things considered in themselves: All parts of creation, including those that are profitable to man, have as their end the glory of God. On this ground, therefore, no distinction between parts of the Lord's Prayer can be made. And yet the reply insists that "the division is not made without reason," the reason being that the other recognizable final cause is the purpose of the agent. Man, the agent of the prayer, may purposely advance God's glory in the first three petitions and separately press for his own profit in the remainder; in other words, the student's distinction is based on the changing motives of the person praying.

Nowell explains, like any good schoolmaster, the etymology of important words. The Greek word for gospel is *evangelion,* 'glad tidings.' *Jesus* is the Hebrew word for the Greek *soter,* the Latin *servator,* and the English *saviour.* The Creed is also called the Symbol of the Apostles because "a symbol by interpretation is a badge, mark, watchword, or token, whereby the soldiers of one side are known from the enemies"—an interpretation that is more likely to promote a bellicose attitude toward other faiths than to foster an ecumenical spirit.

If Dean Nowell was a schoolmaster of his time, he was also typically contemporary in his anti-Romanism. The *Catechism* repudiates him "that esteemeth for holy all the decrees and ordinances of the bishop of Rome," adding with a quick comment on the word *Rome,* that the very addition of the name of one nation contradicts the desired universality of Christendom. The motives of papists are of the very worst: "into this madness are they driven by a blind greediness, and desire to shift and foist the bishop of Rome to be head of the Church in earth, in the stead of Christ." The Roman Catholic practice of reading the Bible in Latin is declared a mockery of God's injunction that his word be preached to all people. Using Latin in their liturgy, the Romans "chatter rather than speak, so far be they from praying. For they play the parrots rather than men, much less Christian men." Images and pictures in Roman Catholic churches are allegedly used to keep the laity from a right understanding of God's word. The master asks: "Have not they[6] then said well, which affirm that images are unlearned men's books?" To which the student replies: "I know not what manner of books they be; but surely concerning God they can teach us nothing but error." Donne echoes this interpretation in the elegy "To his Mistris Going to Bed." The mistress is accused of following the Roman practice of leading man into error; she dresses herself to conceal her body and causes ordinary men to mistake appearance for reality:

> Like pictures, or like books gay coverings made
> For lay-men, are all women thus array'd;
> Themselves are mystick books . . .

Nowell rejects the Roman view of confirmation as a sacrament on the ground that it implies an imperfection in baptism, as if baptized but unconfirmed children are but half Christian. Rome is also attacked for not observing the biblical command to take communion under the two elements of bread and wine, and for upholding the real presence of Christ in those elements. Nowell teaches that the notion of the real presence is so cannibalistic as to "fill them with abhorring that receive the Sacrament." He also, of course, forbids the prayers to saints, giving as one reason that such prayers would "give them, being absent, an understanding of our secret meanings," and as another that "it appeareth nowhere in the word of God that God would have us pray to angels, or to godly men deceased."

Herbert's poem *To all Angels and Saints* expresses a desire to pray to the Virgin Mary: "I would addresse/ My vows to thee most gladly, Blessed Maid." Yet Herbert is reluctant to indulge that craving, and excuses himself on the two grounds stated in Nowell. He is doubtful that the Virgin, being absent, will hear him: ". . . if ye know/ What's done on earth"; secondly, he has as yet found no warrant for his prayer in his "Masters hand," that is, in Scripture. He concludes apologetically: ". . . we are ever ready to disburse/ If any one our Masters hand can show." Herbert's yearning for an older, richer liturgy was strictly bound by the lessons of the *Catechism,* which he valued highly. In *A Priest to the Temple,* he states that catechizing is the parson's first duty and advises that the parson "useth, and preferreth the ordinary Church-Catechism, partly for obedience to Authority, partly for uniformity sake, that the same common truths may be everywhere professed . . . ." [7]

Besides being an experienced schoolmaster and a staunchly antipapist Protestant, Nowell was also an Erastian who firmly believed in the marriage of Church to State. His *Catechism* inculcates strict obedience to civil authority. The explication of the commandment to "Honour thy Father and thy mother" follows the traditional interpretation of "father" and "mother" in that context. God was supposed to have intended, not only one's parents, but also "princes, magistrates, or other superiors, whatsoever they be." Thus the citizen is charged "not only to yield and obey to magistrates, but also to honour and love them." Those who transgress that command by civil rebellion will suffer twice for such ungodliness, for they will bear everlasting pain in the life to come, as well as other, more immediate consequences: "Commonly all such do either continue a most vile and miserable life, or lose it most shamefully, being taken out of it with untimely and cruel death or infamous execution." Regicide is even more execrable than parricide:

> . . . For if it be for every private man a heinous offence to offend his private parents, and parricide to kill them; what shall we say of them that have conspired and borne wicked armour against the commonweal, against their country, the most ancient, sacred, and common mother of us all, which ought to be dearer unto us than ourselves, and for whom no honest man will stick to die to do it good, and against the prince, the father of the country itself, and parent of the commonweal; yea, and to imagine the overthrow, death, and destruction of them whom it is high-treason once to forsake or shrink from? So outrageous a thing can in no wise be expressed with fit name.

Given their early training, it is not surprising that the large majority of Englishmen, the antiroyalist Presbyterians included, recoiled from the regicide of Charles I.

The inevitable problem of the clergyman in an Erastian Church is that he has little means to oppose the abuse of the secular power under whose jurisdiction he ministers to the spiritual needs of the citizens. Consequently, Nowell is highly ambivalent on the question of how much discipline the Church can exercise over the excesses of rich and powerful persons in the realm. He declares that ideally "it shall not be free for any that abideth in that flock publicly to speak or do anything wickedly or in heinous sort without punishment." He follows this, however, with a brief for laxness: "But this discipline since long time past by little and little decaying, as the manners of men be corrupt and out of right course, specially of the rich and men of power, which will needs have impunity and most free liberty to sin and do wickedly, this grave manner of looking to them and of chastisement can hardly be maintained in churches." The *Catechism* thus applies a double standard, and the Church of England paid dearly for this ethically dubious accomodation as the country moved ever closer to the Civil War.

## The law and the gospel

Catechisms were supposed to present essential doctrine. Although centuries of interpretation and debate lay behind each point of dogma of a church, its official catechism was always intended to be no more than a synopsis. The Anglican *Catechism* of Dean Nowell is no exception to that rule. Its author plans the "plaine setting out of truth as not in controversie, without dealing with the strife of confutation."[8] For this very reason, Nowell's little book presents the broadest and clearest survey of religious belief in England under Elizabeth and her early Stuart successors. It is indeed, like most catechisms, brief: a mere 35,000 words in its English translation.

The plain setting out of doctrine begins with a definition of Christian religion as "the true and godly worshipping of God and keeping of his commandments." The source of religion is the word of God, which is contained in the Bible only. Scripture delivers the heavenly doctrine that opens heaven, and to add to Scripture is "intolerable ungodliness." Church councils and assemblies can make no new articles of religion but may only convene to expound "dark places," to solve controversies, or to order the government of the visible Church, the body of believers.

The word of God consists of two parts, the law and the gospel. Accordingly, religion is also divided into two: obedience to the law and faith in the gospel. Scripture occasionally uses other words for "obedience," but this does not change the impact of the law: "For sometime for obedience they set charity, which by the law is required to be perfect toward God and men; and sometime, because we perform neither obedience nor charity such as we ought, they put in place thereof repentance."[9]

Once the basic definitions and divisions have been decided upon, master and student agree to keep the following order: "*first,* to inquire of obedience, which the law requireth; *secondly,* of faith, which looketh to, and embraceth the promises of the gospel; *thirdly,* of invocation and thanksgiving, which two are most nearly joined together; *fourthly,* and lastly of the sacraments and mysteries of God."

Following that order, the master begins to question the student on the obedience to the law. There are many divine orders scattered throughout Scripture, yet all that God requires of man is summed up in the Tables of the Law, the Ten Commandments, which give man the "full and in all points perfect rule of righteousness." The master takes up the points of the Decalogue one by one, questioning the student on the implication of almost every word. Through exhaustive and ingenious explication a series of ten curt *thou-shalt-not*'s is thus transformed into the "perfect rule" of life. The elaborate analysis of each commandment applies three formulae. The first of these is that "one example containeth a generall doctrine"; hence, "thou shalt not steal" condemns

. . . not only those thefts which are punished by men's laws, but also all frauds and deceivings. But none doth offend more heinously against this law, than they that are wont by means of trust to beguile them toward whom they pretend friendship. For they that break faith labour to overthrow the common succor of all men. We are therefore commanded that we deceive no man; that we undermine no man; that we suffer not ourselves to be allured with advantage or gain of buying or selling, to do any wrong; that in trading or buying or selling we seek not wealth unjustly, nor make our profit by untrue and uneven measures and weights, nor increase our riches with sale of slight and deceitful ware.

The second formula implies that any command which restrains man from an overt act also forbids an inward disposition towards it, because God is always chiefly concerned about the affections of the heart. Thus, the eighth commandment not only forbids theft, "but also we are charged to be altogether so minded, that though we were sure to escape unpunished and unespied, yet we would of ourselves forbear from wrong . . . . Therefore all counsels and devices, and especially the very desire to make gain of other's loss, is forbidden by this law." The third formula holds that God's rule against a vice implies an order to practice the contrary virtue in thought and deed; therefore, "thou shalt not steal" also means that man must "endeavour all the ways we may that every man may most speedily come to his own, and safely keep that which he possesseth." By the application of such an analytical method "thou shalt not kill" becomes "thou shalt love thine enemy." Because the law, so interpreted, covers every aspect of human conduct and motivation, Herbert calls it God's "glorious Law" (*Vanitie*).

The *Catechism* teaches explicitly that God's law, as summed up in the Decalogue, is the law of nature; it is "the highest reason . . . by God grafted in the nature of man." And "since the nature of man became stained with sin, although the minds of wise men have been in some sort lightened with the brightness of this natural light, yet in the most part of men this light is so put out, that scarce any sparkles thereof are seen." There would have been no need for God to engrave his law in tables of stone had man's reason and will not been corrupted by the Fall. The explicit promulgation of the law is therefore an act of mercy on God's part, in order that fallen man might know his duty in the course of life. All subsequent laws devised by civil and ecclesiastical authority must be similar to the divine law in motive and purpose: to set weak men on the road to righteousness; and no law that goes counter to the law of God has any moral force. It is this concept of the law of God and nature that Milton uses in his attacks on the legal restrictions imposed by king, bishops, or parliament. Milton's view is thoroughly catechetical when he declares that the law of God is "no other than that law of nature given originally to Adam, and of which a certain remnant, or imperfect illumination, still dwells in the hearts of mankind."[10]

Paradoxically, the "glorious Law" is also the law of death. It promises life to those that abide by it, but threatens death to its transgressors. Theoretically, man can be justified by the law, that is, declared free from the penalty of sin by perfect observance of God's commandments. In practice, however, fallen man is too deeply corrupted to fulfill the entire law. Partial observance will not suffice for justification, for Scripture pronounces damnation on any one who does not obey the law in every point. The *Catechism* therefore concludes that "no mortal man is justified before God by the law"; requiring of imperfect men a perfect righteousness, the law becomes "the ministry of death and damnation." The Father puts the issue in the starkest terms before His heavenly audience in *Paradise Lost:* "Die he [man] or justice must" (III, 210). Vaughan, in "Mans fall, and Recovery," describes the changes of man's ever worsening position under the law, from the understanding granted in paradise to the dark burden of guilt after the Fall, till the verdict of doom implicit in the tables of the law given to Moses:

> Besides I've lost
> A traine of lights, which in those Sun-shine dayes
> Were my sure guides, and only with me stayes
> (Unto my cost,)
> One sullen beame, whose charge is to dispense
> More punishment, than knowledge to my sense;
> Two thousand yeares
> I sojourn'd thus; at last *Jeshuruns* king
> Those famous tables did from *Sinai* bring;
> These swell'd my feares,
> Guilts, trespasses, and all this Inward Awe,
> For sinne tooke strength, and vigour from the Law.

The *Catechism* asks the unavoidable question: What is the divine purpose in delivering a law that is a certain death warrant? God's aim, it is explained, is twofold. First, man must be taught humility. Standing accused under the law, the human heart is moved with sorrow and repentance, and humbly craves strength from God. The law is therefore a harsh medicine that conditions man to seek rightousness from a source other than himself. Secondly, the law is only one half of the Father's design; it is a dramatic preparation for the other part of the divine plan: the illustration of His mercy through the sacrifice of the Son. There are therefore two ways of looking at the law. It is indeed the law of sin and death, and Herbert speaks of "the Laws sowre juice." Yet he also praises its therapeutic power:

> What hath not man sought out and found,
> But his deare God? Who yet his glorious law
> Embosomes in us, mellowing the ground.
> With showres and frosts, with love & aw,
> So that we need not say, Where's this command?
>                                    *Vanitie,* 22–26.

The law prepares the soul to accept the grace of Christ, "Who of the Laws sowre juice sweet wine did make,/ Even God himself being pressed for my sake" (*The Bunch of Grapes*). Thus the law of death is complemented by the promise of life in the gospel, and man's obedience to the first must be accompanied by faith in the second.

Yet, if man is not justified by obedience, neither is he justified by faith. Christ is the only cause of justification. "Thou sayest then," the master recapitulates, "that faith is not the cause but the instrument of justification, for that it embraceth Christ, which is our justification, coupling us with so strait a bond to him, that it maketh us partakers of all his good things." The merits of Christ's redemptive sacrifice are not *earned* by faith in Him, but are merely "imputed" to man. Man can find righteousness only through Christ, and it is solely through His effort that mankind is heir to heaven. Consequently, obedience to the law is still needed after the Redemption because man needs to be continually reminded of his own unworthiness and his dependence on the divine mercy. Vaughan's "The Law, and the Gospel" asks that "I may as well as *Love,* find too thy *fear!*"

From these two points—man's death under the law and his justification through Christ only—it follows that good works have no value in the sight of God. They can contribute nothing to salvation "because they proceed from a faulty and corrupted heart."

Herbert's *Redemption* illustrates the pointlessness of man's own search for salvation: Man cannot buy back his lease or renegotiate his condition—all the work is Christ's and grace is *gratis.* This does not free man from the duty to perform good works; although they do not cause his justification, they are the natural effect thereof. Through God's grace, the soul is newly formed "to the endeavour of innocency and holiness," and hence "good works do stand upon faith as their root." No one is truly faithful who does not shun vice and follow virtue. The most important reason for doing good works is that they form a kind of system of mutual assurance between God and the soul; God, in prompting them, assures the soul of His good will, and the soul, in performing them, returns to God a token of love and faith.

The catechetical doctrine concerning the relationship of the law, the gospel, and good works is helpful for an understanding of Herbert's purpose in *The Temple*. The aim of *The Temple* is to show the road to righteousness, and Herbert pictures with delicate care the total surrender to God that is required for individual holiness. Most of the poems in his marvelous building deal with the soul's repeated attempts and failures to arrive at a "true and lively faith." In *Affliction* (I), the speaker shows his inadequate understanding of the divine plan in his complaint of God's dealings with him. He attributes to himself a place of significance, viewing his service to God as that of a courtier who deserves reward from the king.

> When first thou didst entice to thee my heart,
>     I thought the service brave:
> So many joyes I writ down for my part,
>     Besides what I might have
> Out of my stock of naturall delights,
> Augmented with thy gracious benefits.

The speaker's presumption is manifest in the last two lines of this stanza. Nowell teaches that "by Christ alone we have access to the grace of God. We, receiving this benefit of his free liberality and goodness, have nothing at all to offer or render again to him by way of reward or recompense." Herbert's speaker has the temerity to say that God's "gracious benefits" would augment his own "stock of naturall delights." He does not understand that divine grace can only move in after the soul has emptied itself of pride and vain affections. He has, moreover, been attracted by the mere outward show of the beauty and richness of church appointments:

> I looked on thy furniture so fine,
>     And made it fine to me:
> Thy glorious houshold-stuffe did me entwine,
>     And 'tice me unto thee.
> Such starres I counted mine: both heav'n and earth
> Payd me my wages in a world of mirth.

The speaker has been taken in by the very things the *Catechism* bids one to avoid when it counsels not to "gather together curiously dainty things for banqueting, or precious apparel, or sumptuous household stuff, for pleasure." In his ignorance the speaker believed that he could combine the pleasure of heaven and earth, and he prematurely thought of himself as living in the promised land of "milk and sweetnesses" (line 19). The subsequent tribulations that he records—the loss of friends, health, and hopes for a career—are the inevitable consequences of his ignorance that insisted on having "my wish and way" (line 20). Yet the pains he complains of are, in fact, signs that God cares enough to teach him by trial. The speaker of this poem fails to understand this. He still believes that he can be justified through fulfilling some purpose of his own devising:

> I reade, and sigh, and wish I were a tree;
>   For sure then I should grow
> To fruit or shade: at least some bird would trust
> Her houshold to me, and I should be just.

Man's incapacity to recognize his insignificance before God reappears over and over again. In *Employment* (II) the speaker longs to bring forth his own fruit from a cold and sterile earth:

> Oh that I were an Orenge-tree,
>   That busie plant!
> Then should I ever laden be,
>   And never want
> Some fruit for him that dressed me.

Again, the speaker of *The Pearl* suffers from the same delusion that he is a man of worth, and therefore acceptable to God. Arguing that he knows, after all, the ways of learning, honor, and pleasure, he concludes:

> Therefore not sealed, but with open eyes
> I flie to thee, and fully understand
> Both the main sale, and the commodities;
> With all the circumstances that may move . . . .

Having so presumptuously arranged the price for the sale of his soul, it is in keeping with his character that his final admission of dependence on God should sound like a phrase from a book

of rhetorical "formularies," a mere gesture of humility to persuade
the affection of the party addressed:

> Yet through these labyrinths, not my groveling wit,
> But thy silk twist let down from heav'n to me,
> Did both conduct and teach me, how by it
>   To climbe to thee.

Inevitably, the pride of "The Pearl" is dashed down in the poem
that follows [*Affliction* (IV)]:

> Broken in pieces all asunder,
>   Lord, hunt me not,
>   A thing forgot,
> Once a poore creature, now a wonder,
>   A wonder tortur'd in the space
>   Betwixt this world and that of grace.

When we come to *Sinnes Round,* one meaning of the title is
explicit from the structure of the poem: The stanzas are linked
to illustrate the vicious circle described by evil thoughts, words,
and deeds. Notice, however, that *Sinnes Round* occurs immediately
after *Hope.* The latter poem records the same ailment as did
*Affliction* (I) and *The Pearl,* namely, the presumption of expecting
God's grace in recompense for one's own works:

> I gave to Hope a watch of mine: but he
>   An anchor gave to me.
> Then an old prayer-book I did present:
>   And he an optick sent.
> With that I gave a viall full of tears:
>   But he a few green eares.
> Ah Loyterer! I'le no more, no more I'le bring:
>   I did expect a ring.

The watch is a reminder that Hope has forgotten the speaker for
a long time now; the prayer book represents his continued devotion, and the vial of tears his sorrow. In return he receives the
anchor of steadfastness, a telescope symbolizing his distance from
heaven, and some green ears reminding him of his immaturity.
His rebellious outcry in the last two lines proves that he is still
spiritually unripe: He suffers from the delusion that his offerings
give him the right to expect God's favor. The refusal "I'le no more,

no more I'le bring" is reminiscent of the refusal to serve no more that ends the monologue of *Affliction* (I). *Hope,* therefore, shows the soul revolving back to earlier and similar thoughts of sinning, and *Sinnes Round* follows immediately to underscore that point.

Not understanding his place in God's scheme, the speaker in so many of the poems in *The Temple* prays and complains without effect, for "such as pray doubting and uncertain of their speeding, they do without fruit pour out vain and bootless words" (Nowell). He keeps straying into error, but each failure also refines him and prepares his soul to meet his Maker in humility. Not until he nears the end of the volume does Herbert show the soul as capable of the self-surrender that is the requisite of the true faith. *The Odour* is a humble request that God grant the soul the title of "servant." In the *Forerunners* the "dittie" that fully contents the speaker is the plain phrase "Thou art still my God," and in *The Posie* his motto is *lesse than the least of thy mercies.* The tincture that transforms the dross of life into gold in *The Elixir* is the formula "for thy sake." In the last twenty poems the soul no longer complains; now Herbert clarifies and presents dramatically what the catechism calls the "assured persuasion of mind and stedfast confidence of God's good-will."

We may conclude that Herbert's contemporaries would recognize many nuances of mood and meaning in poems that impress modern readers as being merely verbal variations on one theme. Herbert does not state catechetical doctrine, for the plain reason that he did not need to—his audience would realize that his intention was to transform theory into practical example, to render a finely detailed picture of what, precisely, is demanded for a true and lively faith. He makes it clear that it requires continued care in the remaking of the old man and a return to that "innocency and holiness which we call the newness of life." The final accomplishment of that renewal through surrender is movingly presented in *Love* (III), which closes the main part of *The Temple.* Here, as always in Herbert, the speaker's tone is the mark of his character and spirituality. His language is utterly simple, and being granted entrance into God's company, he confesses his unworthiness of so gracious a benefit. *Love* (III) ends with a mutual surrender: When the soul gives itself over to God, God embraces the soul and becomes its food.

Love bade me welcome: yet my soul drew back,
  Guiltie of dust and sinne.
But quick-ey'd Love, observing me grow slack
  From my first entrance in,
Drew nearer to me, sweetly questioning,
  If I lack'd any thing.

A guest, I answer'd, worthy to be here:
  Love said, You shall be he.
I the unkinde, ungratefull? Ah my deare,
  I cannot look on thee.
Love took my hand, and smiling did reply,
  Who made the eyes but I?

Truth Lord, but I have marr'd them: let my shame
  Go where it doth deserve.
And know you not, sayes Love, who bore the blame?
  My deare, then I will serve.
You must sit down, sayes Love, and taste my meat:
  So I did sit and eat.

## *Obedience:* Paradise Lost

Some modern readers find little clarity in Milton's opening definition of the Fall as "Man's First Disobedience." They are not further enlightened in all the twelve books that follow, because the
poet supplies no other cause for Adam's sin; the words 'obey,'
'obedience,' 'disobey,' and 'disobedience' occur so frequently as to
be a leitmotif of Milton's justification of the ways of God. A good
deal of critical analysis and commentary has attempted to look
beyond Milton's explicit definition in order to find, in the interpretation of Adam's words and action, a more modern and hence,
presumably, a more plausible explanation of sin. One critic blames
Adam's transgression on his gregariousness; another finds him too
intemperate; a third opines that the first husband suffered from
uxoriousness; while a fourth concludes that his failure is un-
reason.[11] Some would be happy to have Satan share part of the
blame, because the poem's answer to the question "Say first what
cause/ Mov'd our Grand Parents" is "Th'infernal Serpent." But
that will not do either. Milton's contemporaries would admit
Satan as a "cause" in a limited sense of that word; he is the
instrumental but not the efficient cause—he is not the agent of
the sin, merely the means whereby it is brought about.

If the repeated stress on obedience is a hindrance for some modern readers of *Paradise Lost,* it aided the appreciation of Milton's contemporaries: Obedience is also a motif of catechetical teaching. Before the law was concretely delivered on Sinai, it was written in Adam's uncorrupted heart. As a visible reminder of that law within, God selected a forbidden tree in Paradise. The tree was not intended as a temptation but as a guide:

> . . . When the Lord God had made this world, he prepared a most finely trimmed garden, and most full of delight and pleasantness, everywhere abounding with all delightful things that might be wished. Herein the Lord God, for a certain singular good-will placed man, and allowed him the use of all things, only he forbad him the fruit of the tree of knowledge of good and evil, threatening him with death, if he once tasted of it. For reason it was, that man having received so many benefits, should, in so far obeying, shew himself willingly obedient to the commandment of God, and that being contented with his own estate, he should not, being himself a creature, advance himself higher against the will of his Creator.

Adam disobeys an admittedly arbitrary order, but its arbitrariness has nothing whatsoever to do with its validity: The forbidden fruit is merely the symbol of the allegiance due to the Creator.

Genesis declares that Adam was made in the image of God—an obscure comparison, to say the least, because it likens an unknown entity, man in paradise, to another even more mysterious being, God in heaven. Scripture does not clarify the likeness between God and man until Christ comes to fulfill His redemptive mission. Nowell teaches that Adam's original image "hath been most evidently shewed in Christ our new Adam, and whereof in us there now scarcely appear any sparkles." Christ, the second Adam, redeems the disobedience of the first by giving His life in obedience to the justice exacted by the law. The catechism underscores that lesson by a reference to the Apostle Paul: "And being found in fashion as a man, he humbled himself, and became obedient unto death, even the death of the cross" (Phil. 2:8).

The gospel is the *Evangelion,* the glad tidings of Christ, because it gives assurance that He has expiated man's disobedience to the law. With Him, man's sins were crucified and man's old self buried in the grave; with Him also, man is risen to a new life. Christ's act of expiation in obedience to the law does not free man from the obligation to be obedient. On the contrary, the redemption re-enforces that duty. Christ revealed what man must do to return again to a state of grace and favor, to restore in himself the image of God. Jesus is the new Adam, the exemplar to follow, and His 'obedience unto death' is required of all men. This is the lesson that Adam learns in the closing books of *Paradise Lost:* how to prosper in obedience, taught by the example of his redeemer yet to come. The *Catechism* declares that, as Christ is the head of the Church, "the universal number of the faithful," the latter must be "in all things obedient to Christ" because He has received dominion over all men, angels, and all things:

> . . . And hereby are all the godly put in mind, that they are not at their own liberty, but that both in their bodies and souls, and in their life and death, they are wholly subject to their Lord, to whom they ought to be obedient and serviceable in all things, as most faithful servants.

Both the law and the gospel demand obedience; but the first exacts the penalty of death, the second changes that penalty by offering a new life after the death of the body. Adam's disobedience gave man the bitter taste of mortality; mortal he must remain, but Christ's exemplary obedience restores his hope of immortality.

The gospel also lays claim to continued obedience on the ground that man is more than God's creature: He is his child. The stress on the affiliation, in the etymological sense of that word, between God and man is one of the differences between the Old and the New Testaments. The *Catechism* explains that the title God the Father has three meanings: He is Father to the Son; He is the Father of man because he brought that creature forth; but

> the other cause is of greater value, namely for that he hath heavenly begotten us again through the Holy Ghost, and by faith in his true and natural Son Jesus Christ he hath adopted us his children, and through the same Christ hath given us his kingdom, and the inheritance of everlasting life.

Man is God's child and heir under the terms of the New Testament. The latter is legally the new will of God. Jeremy Taylor explains that "The Gospels are Christ's Testament; and the Epistles are the Codicils annex'd."[12] This interpretation of 'testament' finds its authority in Scripture itself. The Epistle to the

Hebrews, discussing the ritual of purification of the old Mosaic priesthood, concludes:

> For if the blood of bulls and of goats, and the ashes of an heifer sprinkling the unclean, sanctifieth to the purifying of the flesh:
> How much more shall the blood of Christ, who through the eternal Spirit offered himself without spot to God, purge your conscience from dead works to serve the living God?
> And for this cause he is the mediator of the new testament, that by means of death, for the redemption of the transgressions that were under the first testament, they which are called might receive the promise of eternal inheritance.
> For where a testament is, there must also of necessity be the death of the testator.
> For a testament is of force after men are dead: otherwise it is of no strength at all while the testator liveth.
>
> 9:13–17

In the Mosaic ritual the sprinkling of the blood of animals was a mere symbol of man's desire to be cleansed of sin. The Old Testament is therefore only the Testament of promise, to be fulfilled by the New, which is sealed by the death of its testator, Christ. This Son of God is also the Son of Man, and through their kinship with Him all men carry "the name of children by right of adoption." Hence, when the *Catechism* under the heading of "The Order of Prayer and Thanksgiving" diligently examines the weight of every word, the student finds "great pith in the use of this one name Father." God prefers the affection of "Father" to the dignity and majesty of "Lord" or "King." If indeed "sure trust of obtaining" is the foundation of prayer, there is no better way to evidence that trust than by "Father," which is "the sweetest name on earth." God will give to men "as to his children a most rich inheritance of his fatherly name." It is worth noting that the tone of many of Herbert's later poems is childlike, that for Vaughan and Traherne childhood is the symbol of spiritual recovery, and that Herrick's *Noble Numbers* shows a deliberate simplicity of spirit.[13]

Man's childhood under the New Testament re-enforces the need for obedience. Nowell teaches that men must please God "as becometh obedient children" and should come to prayer with "that love, reverence, and obedience, which is due to the heavenly Father from his children." Mankind must desire god's glory and the fulfillment of His will. Not that God needs man's assistance for the realization of His design, but He desires man's consent; His children should obey Him "not only with contented, but also with gladsome hearts." There is, after all, no occasion for resistance: God always orders for the best, and there is no difference between what He 'orders' or commands, and what He 'orders' or arranges. His entire creation is an ideal order in both senses of the word. When Nowell's student is asked why the Lord's Prayer asks that His will be done "in earth as it is in heaven," he answers:

> . . . as in heaven there is no rebellion, so in earth also there be none anywhere found that will or dare resist and strive against the holy will of God. Yea, and when we behold the sun and moon, and other stars which we see in the heaven, to be carried with continual motion and perpetual stirring, and with their beams to lighten the earth by the will of God, we behold an example of obedience set forth for us to follow.

Vaughan's "The Constellation" is a paraphrase of this passage, a meditation on those "Fair, order'd lights," which complains of man's unwillingness to seek their *Obedience, Order, Light:*

> With what exact obedience do you move
>    Now beneath, and now above,
> And in your vast progressions overlook
>    The darkest night, and closest nook!
>
> .    .    .    .    .    .    .
>
> Settle, and fix our hearts, that we may move
>    In order, peace, and love,
> And taught obedience by thy whole Creation,
>    Become an humble, holy nation.

The illumination of God's design in His two books, Scripture and Nature, is necessary for fallen man whose hardened heart has to be taught its dependence on God. Adam in paradise had no need of catechetical instruction. His very appearance showed the image of his maker: "Truth, Wisdom, Sanctitude severe and pure,/ Severe but in true filial freedom plac't" (*Paradise Lost*, IV, 293–294). The seeming paradox in "filial freedom" sums up the ideal relationship between man and God. Adam was free as the child is free: It exists in its own right but depends for its life on the parent. In that relationship, obedience is not a virtue but the recognition of an inevitable and natural bond. Adam's sin was so heavy in its consequences because it was unnatural. In tasting the fruit he did not merely transgress a divine command; he denied his origin and ruined the natural order.

Milton's early audience needed no explanation of the Fall other than "First Disobedience." *Paradise Lost,* like all great epics, sums up the values of the society that nurtured its author; the epic poet presents a communal attitude.[14] The grandeur of this epic is specifically Miltonic in style, but impersonal in content. Unlike many a modern writer, Milton does not set out to differentiate his views from those of his contemporaries. The doctrine espoused is inclusive, meant to embrace the largest possible audience. Milton's readers would have been most surprised had he termed the Fall other than "First Disobedience."

The word "First" deserves the rhythmical stress it receives in the opening line of the poem. After the first transgression, disobedience has been habitual, a continued state of spiritual degeneracy. In its analysis of that primal act, *Paradise Lost* actually describes the awful consequences of disobedience for human life on earth, and the condition of disobedient men. Put in logical terms, Milton's definition of the Fall is not genetic but causative; it does not describe the origin, but rather the product: "the Fruit" that "brought Death into the World, and all our woe."

For Milton, as for his contemporaries, the principle of obedience was axiomatic and therefore not in need of elaboration. The same is true of the Fall: Its fact was so incontrovertibly established that no poet would have made it the *end* of his meditative exploration. Adam's sin was the beginning of history as Milton's audience knew it, and it is the starting point of *Paradise Lost.* Rightly understood, that epic does not explain what makes Satan, or Adam, or mankind, disobedient, but what disobedience makes of Satan, Adam, and mankind. The explanation includes an ideal picture of what might have been—the happiness of Eden—in order to move man towards what he may still attain through imitating the obedience of Christ: the possession of a paradise within. *Paradise Lost* pursues the end of rhetoric, the improvement of the audience. It instructs the reader how to counter the effects of the Fall. That he was fallen was obvious; he found incontrovertible evidence of that in his own heart, the circumstances of his life, and the history of the world.

## Literary echoes

The parallels traced between Herbert and Milton on the one hand, and Nowell's *Catechism* on the other, are not meant to serve as proof of 'influence.' The intention is merely to show that the *Catechism* is a useful synopsis of the theological patrimony of the seventeenth century, and may enlighten a modern reader as he studies the religious literary art of that age. Much that seems eccentric at first glance was, on the evidence of Nowell's little book, generally accepted.

Time and again the perusal of the *Catechism* reminds us of one detail or another in the works of the metaphysicals and Milton. One cause of these associations is that both the *Catechism* and the religious literature of the age use biblical diction and imagery. Among the most familiar metaphors are those of glass and of growth. We behold, says Nowell, God's graces in outward elements "as it were in certain glasses," and the entire creation is "the glass of God." The man of dead faith is called "a dry and dead stock." Sometimes the *Catechism* develops a biblical image into an expanded conceit, as in its description of the effect of original sin: "out of the root and stock corrupted, there sprung forth corrupted branches, that conveyed also their corruption into the other twigs springing out of them"; and occasionally we encounter an image of Herbertian simplicity and directness, as when God's reign is called "the barn and granary of the kingdom of Heaven."

Now and then the literary echoes are more striking. Nowell declares that "the wits of men are too dull to understand what is expedient for them, and the desires of their hearts are so blind and wild, that they not only need a guide whom they may follow, but also bridles to restrain them"—a passage that recalls Herbert's *The Collar.* Another catechetical statement, explaining that God gives us His benefits "from the springhead of his divine liberality, as it were by certain guiding of water-courses," may well have been the source for the title of Herbert's *The Water-course.* Nowell's description of the declining worth of man's works of godliness is similar to Vaughan's rendering of the corruption of religion:

. . . For though they be derived from the Spirit of God, as little streams from the spring-head, yet of our flesh, that mingleth itself with them, in the doing by the way, they receive corruption as it were by infection, like as a river, otherwise pure and clear, is troubled and mudded with mire and slime, wherethrough it runneth.

Vaughan's "Religion" has:

> . . . Religion is a Spring
> That from some secret, golden Mine
> Derives her birth, and thence doth bring
> Cordials in every drop, and Wine;
>
> But in her long, and hidden Course
> Passing through the Earths darke veines,
> Growes still from better unto worse,
> And both her taste, and colour staines,
>
>          .     .     .     .     .     .     .
>
> So poison'd, breaks forth in some Clime,
> And at first sight doth many please,
> But drunk, is puddle, or meere slime
> And 'stead of Phisick, a disease . . . .

A reading of the *Catechism* may save us from making unwarranted assumptions about the psychology of seventeenth-century religious authors. There is no reason to wonder at the use of erotic terms in the description of the love of God for the soul. The schoolboy was taught the validity and the aptness of such terminology. Asked to explain why the Bible calls God "jealous," he answers that this is for "a most just reason"; the soul's relationship to God is like

> . . . that bond, as it were, of a holy marriage, wherein to God, the faithful husband, our souls, as chaste spouses, are coupled; whose chastity standeth in this, to be dedicated to God alone, and to cleave wholly to him, like as on the other side our souls are said to be defiled with adultery, when they swerve from God to idolatry or superstition. And how much more heartily the husband loveth the wife, and the chaster he is himself, so much is he more grievously displeased with his wife when she breaketh her faith.

The student did not, of course, take such comparisons literally. He was trained to distinguish between many variations of figurative expression. In matters of religion he was mindful of the carefully inculcated ground rule that whenever man speaks of the mysteries of faith, his words are merely tentative approaches towards truth: "because we speak of God among men, we do in some sort [speak] after the manner of men." On the other hand, God's language in Scripture, although figurative, has to be thoroughly weighed because His figures contain His truth; they are "not empty or deceitful, but such as have the truth of the things themselves joined and knit unto it." God would not mislead man by casual or "vain" figures. The sophistication required of the student in his analysis of God's word is clear from the catechetical commentary on the phrase from the Lord's Prayer, "who art in Heaven." Although heaven is not a place, the figurative language is nevertheless true:

> As heaven with round and endless circuit containeth all things, compasseth the earth, hemmeth in the seas, neither is there anything or place that is not environed and enclosed with the roominess of heaven; and it is on every side wide and open, and always so present to all things, that all things universally are placed, as it were, in sight thereof: so we thereby understand that God, possessing the tower of heaven, therewith also holdeth the governance of all things, is each where present, seeth, heareth, and ruleth all things . . . . God is also therefore said to be in heaven, because that same highest and heavenly region doth most royally shine, and is garnished with his divine and excellent works. Moreover by God reigning in heaven is declared that he is in eternal and highest felicity, while we as yet in earth, expulsed from our country, like children disherited from their father's goods, live miserably and wretchedly in banishment. It is as much therefore to say, that God is in heaven, as if I should call him heavenly and altogether divine; this is to say, incomprehensible, most high, most mighty, most blessed, most good, most great.

No one who had received this kind of training would have made an issue of the vague and shifting delineations of God's universe in *Paradise Lost*. On the contrary, blueprints and schemas would have offended Milton's contemporaries. The Miltonic *vague* was not only inevitable in view of the poet's matter, but also a source of delight for the reader. It stimulated him to discover for himself how Milton's figures had the truth of things "joined and knit" unto them.

# Chapter Six

# *Typology: Divine Hieroglyphics*

### *Type, prophecy and allegory*[1]

Oh that I knew how all thy lights combine,
    And the configurations of their glorie!
    Seeing but onely how each verse doth shine,
But all the constellations of the storie.
This verse marks that, and both do make a motion
    Unto a third, that ten leaves off doth lie:
    Then as dispersed herbs do watch a potion,
These three make up some Christians destinie:
Such are thy secrets, which my life makes good,
    And comments on thee: for in ev'ry thing
    Thy words do finde me out, & parallels bring,
And in another make me understood.
    Starres are poore books, & oftentimes do misse:
    This book of starres lights to eternal blisse.
                    *The Holy Scriptures* II

In the quest for holiness, as described in *The Temple*, the soul finds comfort, hope, and even assurance in God's word. Scripture is the revelation of His grand design. Yet the very grandeur of the divine plan is an obstacle to man's comprehension of it. The Christian must apply himself with utmost care to the study of the Bible if he is ever to begin to understand God's direction of the world and of man. Herbert aptly compares Scripture to an astronomical map of the heavens. Men read their destiny in the stars, and mariners set their courses by them; the Bible is the revelation of man's eternal destiny and charts the way by which to attain it. Yet Scripture, like an astronomical map, requires a competent interpreter. The mariner determines his position by marking the constellations of the stars above him; similarly, man can only understand his place in God's universe through a study of the configurations of various biblical passages: "This verse marks that, and both do make a motion/ Unto a third, that ten leaves off doth lie." The "leaves" of Scripture remind Herbert of the leaves of plants and suggest another comparison to illustrate the difficulty of biblical study: God's hidden operation in Scripture is like the way in which "dispersed herbs do watch a potion." Scattered herbs guard their secret, curative powers until the subtle chemist extracts these effects and combines them into a medicinal 'potion.' In the same way, both a knowledge of biblical details and a discreet discerning of their interrelationships is needed to obtain Scripture's healing power. "Parallels," in line eleven, returns the reader to the earlier metaphor of Scripture as a chart. As distances in the heavens are measured by means of parallels of declination, latitude, and altitude, so man's distance from or closeness to God can be known through biblical parallels. Obviously one verse cannot be called a parallel until one finds a second that is parallel to it. Yet by "parallels" Herbert does not mean that one should merely discover passages in Scripture that declare the same thing, for it is also obvious that such parallelisms would be mere repetitions incapable of enhancing man's understanding of his intended course through life. What Herbert means by scriptural parallels are instructive correspondences in which a second and third passage bring additional knowledge: "Thy words do finde me out, & parallels bring,/ *And in another make me understood.*" In brief, Herbert urges a typological approach to the Bible.

The New Testament frequently alludes to the Old. The first Christians were Jews, and those Gentiles early converted to Christianity were strongly influenced by Judaism. The sacred texts of the synagogue were also read at the meetings of members of the primitive Church. The writers of the New Testament assumed therefore that their audience was familiar with the Old. The most significant link they forge between the two Covenants is the correspondence between the life of Christ and the message of the prophets.

The messianic prophecies begin with God's intention to defeat the serpent through the seed of woman (Gen. 3:15), and are made more specific by His promise to Abraham, Isaac, and Jacob that in their posterity all the nations of the earth shall be blessed. The psalms and the books of the prophets supply further details about the manner of Israel's future delivery from bondage. At the time of Christ, rabbinical commentary had decided which passages in the sacred writings were prophetic, and in the gospels Christ makes use of them to illustrate that He is the announced Messiah. His Sermon on the Mount declares: "Think not that I am come to destroy the law or the prophets: I am not come to destroy but to fulfill" (Mat. 5:17). Reading in the synagogue of Nazareth one of the prophecies of Isaiah (61:1–2), He concludes: "This day is this scripture fulfilled in your ears" (Luke 4:21).

The Old Testament prophecies are God's specific instructions that He guides the course of the world. His promises are declarations of His intent to demonstrate His power over all things. They are the first half of His proof of omnipotence; the other half is their eventual fulfillment in the New Testament. The prophecies and their realization establish therefore a system of overt correspondences between the two parts of the Christian Bible.

Early Christian exegesis discovered, however, a system of hidden correspondences as well, and held that Christ Himself traced such secret patterns between the Pentateuch and His own mission when He found new meanings in the brazen serpent, the water of Jacob's well, the manna in the desert, and the Temple of Jerusalem. After God had punished the rebellious Israelites by sending fiery serpents among them, Moses prayed for an end to divine vengeance and received a prescription to cure snakebite: He was to make a serpent of brass, raise it upon a pole, and "every one that is bitten, when he looketh upon it, shall live" (Num. 21:5–9). Traditional exegesis held that Christ referred to His being lifted up on the cross when He said: "And as Moses lifted up the serpent in the wilderness, even so must the Son of man be lifted up: that whosoever believeth in him should not perish, but have everlasting life" (John 3:14–15). Christ promises the woman of Samaria that, instead of the water of Jacob's well, He will give her the water of everlasting life (John 4:14). When the people ask Him for proof of His divine mission, as Moses had proved his leadership by bringing manna for food,

Christ answers that He is the true bread from heaven (John 6:32). And after driving the money lenders out of the Temple of Jerusalem, He speaks of His own body as the temple in a prophecy of His Resurrection: "Destroy this temple and in three days I will raise it up" (John 2:19). Christ uncovers these secret correspondences between the Hebrew past and the future of His making in the Gospel of John: That evangelist makes of Christ the first practitioner of typology.

*Typos,* from the Greek τύπτεῖν, 'to strike,' may mean the impression left by a blow: The word is used in the New Testament for the marks of the nails left in Christ's hands (John 20:25); it may refer to a statue hammered out by the sculptor (Acts 7:43); it may also signify the 'mold' after which things are made or done (Heb. 8:5), and, by extension, 'moral example' (I Tim. 14:12). But in Rom. 5:14 'type' is used in its strict theological sense when Paul calls Adam the *typos* of Christ, translated in the Authorized Version as "the figure of him that was to come." In biblical typology type is defined as a detail in the Old Testament that foreshadows its antitype in the New. The detail may be a person (Adam, Melchizedek, and Moses are types of Christ); it may be an event (the Passover and the crossing of the Red Sea foreshadow the Redemption); or it can be an institution (the Levitical priesthood and the ritual of the old temple are figures of the blessings of the spiritual priesthood of Christ).

The difference between type and prophecy is that a type is not recognizable until its antitype is known. The very translation of *typos* as 'shadow' or 'figure' implies that its significance eluded those who lived before the completion of that which is but dimly outlined in the type. Prophecy looks forward, from Old Testament promise to fulfillment in the gospels; typology looks back, from the New Testament completion of God's design to its hidden prefigurations in the Old. The New Testament offers, therefore, two kinds of proof of God's guidance of history. The first kind is the fulfillment of His explicit prophecies; the second is the correspondence between New Testament antitypes and the types of the Old. Like prophecy, typology is based on the belief in divine omnipotence over human affairs, but typological proofs are strictly *ex post facto* explanations.

Typology received its impetus from the earliest controversy in the primitive Church. The first Jewish converts to Christianity held that the messianic Redemption applied to them only, and even after it had been decided that Gentiles might enter into the New Convenant, the question arose as to the conditions they had to fulfill in order to be included among the elect. The Judaizing Christian believed that the old Mosaic law had to be observed by all converts. The Apostle Paul, the champion of the Gentiles, expressed himself forcefully against the old law. He insisted that the Mosaic law was only a past foreshadowing of the new order and should hence be abrogated. Faith in God was Paul's only requisite for conversion. Abraham, who lived before the Redemption, was accounted righteous by God (Gen. 15:6), not because he submitted to circumcision, but because he believed in Him:

> He therefore that ministereth to you the Spirit, and worketh miracles among you, doeth he it by the works of the law, or by the hearing of faith?
> Even as Abraham believed God, and it was accounted to him for righteousness.
> Know ye therefore that they which are of faith, the same are the children of Abraham.
> And the scripture, foreseeing that God would justify the heathen through faith, preached before the gospel unto Abraham, saying In thee shall all nations be blessed.
> So then they which be of faith are blessed with faithful Abraham.
>
> Gal. 3:5–9

The faithful Abraham, who was righteous before "the law which was four hundred and thirty years after" (Gal. 3:17), is for Paul the type of all the followers of Christ, who are granted righteousness through faith. In I Cor. 10:1–4, Paul declares that baptism and communion are antitypes foreshadowed in Hebrew history:

> Moreover, brethren, I would not that ye should be ignorant, how that all our fathers were under the cloud, and all passed through the sea;
> And were all baptized unto Moses in the cloud and in the sea;
> And did all eat the same spiritual meat;
> And did all drink the same spiritual drink; for they drank of that spiritual Rock that followed them: and that Rock was Christ.

Moses had to use a veil to cover "the glory of his countenance" because "the children of Israel could not stedfastly behold" him (II Cor. 3:7); Paul interprets Moses' veil as the type of the full revelation of God's glory in Christ. The veil was God's sign that the Hebrews were merely allowed to see only the dim reflection of His divinity.

The Epistle to the Hebrews contains more examples of typological interpretation than any other book of the New Testament. The letter is of uncertain authorship and is probably addressed to Jewish Christians who still remembered and took pride in the grandeur of their old faith, the glory of the Temple of Jerusalem, and the beauty of the ancient ritual. The author's approach to the Hebrew past is more sympathetic than that of Paul, who minimized the Hebrew tradition because he saw it as a *mere* prefiguration. The tone of the author of Hebrews conveys that Jewish converts may justifiably be proud of their ancient heritage *because* their past was God's intended foreshadowing of a greater glory. Moses was indeed a type, a servant in the house of which Christ is Master, but he was also a "testimony of those things which were to be spoken after" (Heb. 3:4). The beauty of the old temple and all the splendid memories of the Jewish past are still admirable because they are "patterns of things in the heavens" and "figures of the true." The typological interpretation, especially as it is applied in Hebrews, was a means of preserving the significance of the entire Old Testament, not merely of those parts that were overtly prophetic.

The influence of neo-Platonism, as it was taught in Alexandria, is strongly present in Hebrews, for the writer of the letter contrasts shadowy reflections with the world of transcendental reality. The latter is the place of "heavenly things," "the House of God," "the genuine Tabernacle," "the City which hath the foundations," "the fatherland," "the heavenly Jerusalem." In Hebrews the religion of the Old Testament is a shadowy pattern, the truth of which is revealed to the Christian in the clearer images of the New, but the full revelation of God's design will occur only in the world to come. The typology of the Gospel of John and the letters of Paul compares the Old Testament types with their New Testament fulfillment, but the typology of Hebrews divides the manifestation of God's truth among three levels. For example, Joshua leading the people of Israel into Canaan, the "rest" promised by God to the ancient Jews (Ex. 33:14), foreshadowed the rest brought to the souls of men by Christ's redemptive sacrifice; the peace of Christ in turn prefigures the final rest in Heaven (4:3–11). And Melchizedek, the mysterious figure who was a priest of God and placed over Abraham long before the institution of the Levitical priesthood, prefigured the non-Levitical but effective priesthood of Christ, whose eternal priesthood we will understand when we enter with Him in His Sanctuary, the presence of the Father in heaven (7:1–3).

The ingenious typology of Hebrews resembles, in derivation and practice, the other effect of Alexandrian teachings on biblical exegesis, the medieval theory of the manifold sense of Scripture. Applying to the Bible the principle that earlier Alexandrian scholarship had applied to Homer, namely, that whatever is not educationally useful is to be interpreted figuratively, Origen explained that every biblical detail expresses simultaneously a literal, moral, and spiritual truth. Origen's method of explication was passed on, through the Church Fathers, to Pope Gregory the Great, who promulgated the view that Scripture has a fourfold sense: historical, moral, allegorical, and anagogic. For instance, the historical Temple of Jerusalem is allegorically the Church on earth; morally, it is the individual believer, and anagogically (or mystically), it is the final communion of saints in heaven.

The allegorical interpreters in the Middle Ages, although accepting the historicity of biblical events, did not really derive their exegesis from the literal sense of the Bible. Their explications were often capricious and, in eager pursuit of the spirit, readily ignored the letter. In contrast, a typological interpretation must respect the literal, historical truth of Scripture. Typology is devoted to the discovery of God's direction of human history. The literal truth of the type is therefore of the utmost importance; although the type is a shadow that prefigures the future, its validity as type depends on its being historically real. The typologist is not allowed to rearrange and reinterpret according to his own insights, and typology does not deliver a neat system of point-by-point correspondences in the manner of the allegorist. Types and antitypes are like shifting signals, scattered by God with apparent casualness throughout Scripture and to be found out by the diligent student of His word. Hence Herbert's opening prayer in *H. Scriptures* II:

"Oh that I knew how all thy lights combine,/ And the configurations of their glorie!"

Although the Reformation rejected the medieval method of the four senses and urged a return to the literal meaning of the Bible, typology survived.[2] When Donne says that the reader must heed the literal sense of Scripture, he does not, as his sermons clearly show, exclude the practice of typological interpretation. Donne includes under his definition of 'literal sense' the meaning intended by God.[3] It follows that typology must be retained for the very reason that God Himself, through the writers of the New Testament, draws the reader's attention to the secret but marvelous Old Testament prefigurations of His redemptive scheme; Herbert says of the history of the Jews under the law: "Their storie pennes and sets us down" (*The Bunch of Grapes*).

In the seventeenth century the Old Testament types were known through the study of the Bible, the Book of Common Prayer, and the lessons of the catechism. Nowell's student repeatedly makes use of typological interpretation. The master, for example, asks why the Decalogue should not refer to the Israelites alone, because God's introduction declares: "Hear, O Israel, I am the Lord thy God, which brought thee out of the land of Egypt, out of the house of bondage." The student answers to this that the pharaoh of Egypt is the figure of the devil ready to oppress the Christian, and that Moses' rescue of the Israelites from bodily bondage is a type of Christ's delivery of all His faithful followers from the bondage of sin. If the people of Israel are the type of the Christians to come, it follows that the law applies to both Israelite and Christian. The catechetical discussion of baptism treats that sacrament as the antitype of the Old Testament circumcision. The latter was the "visible sign" by which God showed himself to be the "Father of young children and of the seed of his people." Yet, although "Moses and all the prophets do testify that circumcision was a sign of repentance," it did not grant forgiveness of sin. In the New Testament, the water of baptism is the visible sign of the Christian's adoption as child of God, but baptism is more powerful than circumcision because the sacrament is a "seal and pledge of the forgiveness of sins." Elsewhere, the catechism asks why the Bible should accord to Christ (literally, "the anointed") the titles of king, priest, and prophet, even though He never received the anointing that the Hebrews used to require for each of these offices. The pupil answers that Christ needed no anointing with oil because he was anointed "with much more excellent oil; namely with the most plentiful grace of the Holy Ghost . . . of which heavenly anointing that outward anointing was but a shadow." Nowell's students knew that the relationship between type and antitype is one of simultaneous difference and likeness. After quoting the fourth commandment, to keep the Sabbath holy, the master asks if Christians must, like the Jews, abstain from *all* labor on that day. In the answer, the pupil discerns "a double consideration. For insomuch as it containeth a ceremony, and requireth only outward rest, it belonged peculiarly to the Jews, and hath not the force of a continuing and eternal law. But now, by the coming of Christ, as the other shadows of Jewish ceremonies are abrogated, so is this law also in this behalf abridged." The word 'Sabbath' means rest and expresses "a certain form and figure of the spiritual rest" of Heaven, for which the faithful prepare themselves by diligently attending to religion and godliness on Sunday. More poetically, Herbert calls Sunday "the next worlds bud," and prays

> O let me take thee at the bound,
> Leaping with thee from sev'n to sev'n,
> Till that we both, being toss'd from earth
> Flie hand in hand to heav'n.
> *Sunday,* 60–64

## The spiritual temple of Herbert

*Lord, my first fruits present themselves to thee;*
*Yet not mine neither: for from thee they came,*
*And must return. Accept of them and me,*
*And make us strive, who shall sing best thy name.*
*Turn their eyes hither, who shall make a gain:*
*Theirs, who shall hurt themselves or me, refrain.*

The dedication of Herbert's *The Temple* combines two biblical sources, the one Mosaic, the other Pauline. In Deut. 26:1–2 Moses commands that the Israelites, after crossing the river Jordan and arriving in the Promised Land, shall make a sacrifice to God of the fruit of their harvest: "And it shall be, when thou art come

into the land which the Lord thy God giveth thee for an inheritance, and possessest it, and dwellest therein; that thou shalt
take of the first of all the fruit of the earth, which thou shalt bring
of thy land that the Lord thy God giveth thee, and shalt go unto
the place the Lord thy God shall choose to place his name there."
The crossing of the river Jordan is a type of the redemption of
mankind through Christ, whose sacrifice on Calvary is the antitype
of all Mosaic sacrifices. In I Cor. 15:23 Paul speaks of "Christ
the first fruits." After Calvary no external sacrifice of propitiation
is necessary or possible, and the only offering the Christian can
bring is the fruit of praise: "By him [Christ] therefore let us offer
the sacrifice of praise to God continually, that is the fruit of our
lips giving thanks to his name" (Heb. 13:15). Moses' place "which
the Lord thy God shall choose to place his name there" is the
old Temple of Jerusalem. The latter is also abolished, because all
that is needed for the Christian's sacrifice of praise is the inward
temple of the thankful heart.

The first part of *The Temple*, "The Church-porch," is a 'sprinkling' of moral counsels and the antitype of the sprinkling of animal
blood in the Mosaic ritual.[4] Then the reader enters "The
Church," the main body of *The Temple*, and encounters a hieroglyph, shaped in such a way that it visually represents the referent
of its title, *The Altar*. However, the form does not represent the
altar or communion table in a Christian church; it gives instead
a picture of the ancient Hebrew altar, a sacrificial stone resting
upon a pillar and base. The shape of the poem is that of the
*typical* altar, but the words describe its New Testament antitype:
"A broken Altar, Lord, thy servant reares/ Made of a heart, and
cemented with teares." The purpose of this altar is to "praise thy
Name," and it will only be agreeable to Heaven through the
sacrifice of Christ: "O let thy blessed Sacrifice be mine,/ And
sanctifie this Altar to be Thine." *The Altar* is logically followed by
*Sacrifice*, in which Christ recounts the sufferings of His Passion,
contrasting His infinite love with man's unrelenting sinfulness.
The complaint of Christ prompts the soul to a vain attempt to
offer up a sacrifice of its own in *The Thanksgiving*. Forgetful of the
biblical injunction that the Christian can only offer praise, the
soul attempts to compete with the love of God: "Surely I will revenge me on thy love,/ And trie who shall victorious prove."

The poems that follow (from *The Reprisall* to *Easter*) are meditations on the graciousness of Christ and man's unworthiness;
they correct the soul's misunderstanding of its participation in
the Redemption. It is not until the hieroglyphical *Easter-wings*
that the soul recognizes that victory belongs to Christ alone. Man
can but "sing this day thy victories," and only by attaching himself to Christ may he "feel this day thy victorie." The lesson of
*Easter-wings* returns us to the doctrine of *The Altar:* The altar of
the heart is sanctified by the sacrifice of Christ only, and serves
no other purpose than to offer thankful praise.

The most significant text for understanding Herbert's antitypical purpose in the architectural design of *The Temple* is that
of I Peter 2:5: "Ye also, as lively stones, are built up a spiritual
house, an holy priesthood, to offer up spiritual sacrifices, acceptable to God by Jesus Christ." In the poems whose titles refer to
details within an actual church (*Church-monuments, Church-musick,
Church-lock and key, The Church-floore* and *The Windows*) Herbert uses
the externals of the building as types that have their antitypes
within man. After these meditations on the soul as a spiritual
house, the poet sums up, in *Trinitie Sunday,* his understanding of
the means and the purpose of his being: Man is the consequence
of the threefold operation of the Trinity, of the Father, Who
creates, of the Son, Who redeems, and of the Spirit, Who sanctifies
him:

> Lord, who hast form'd me out of mud,
> And hast redeem'd me through thy bloud,
> And sanctifi'd me to do good . . . .

The poem ends with the prayer "That I may runne, rise, rest
with thee." This line is analyzed and applied in the sequence of
poems that follow it. *Content, The Quidditie, Humilitie, Frailtie, Constancie,* and *Affliction* (III) all examine how the soul must *runne* its
race. They study the relationship between the Christian and the
world, and are linked by repetitions of diction and argument. If
man is formed out of mud, the world's gifts are only *fair dust*
(*Frailtie* line 14). Man therefore has no need of a "crown" (*Content* line 15, *The Quidditie* line 1), a "gay suit" (*The Quidditie*
line 2), nor of "gay weeds" (*Frailtie* line 14). The soul must try
not to run after the world when "it runnes bias from his will"

(*Constancie* line 32); rather it ought to "cease discoursing" (literally, cease 'running away,' *Content* line 33). The *Quidditie* declares that a verse is "no point of honour," and *Constancie* asks for honesty instead; *Affliction* (III) echoes both these poems:

> Thy life on earth was grief, and thou art still
> Constant unto it, making it to be
> A point of honour, now to grieve in me.

Only through imitating the example of Christ's life in this world may the soul expect to "rise" to Heaven in *The Starre,* there to "rest" with God in *Sunday.*

The entry of *Avarice* after *Sunday* seems at first unusual, but its position is again calculated. The poems that studied the relationship between this world and the next culminate in *Sunday* with a glimpse of heavenly bliss. The Christian can now clearly see the difference between the two worlds and accordingly defines money, extracted from the earth, as the "bane of blisse." At the same time, *Avarice* introduces a sequence of poems dealing with the Incarnation—"Thou hast but two rare cabinets full of treasure,/ The *Trinitie,* and *Incarnation*"(*Ungratefulnesse* lines 6–7). Money is false gold, found "poore and dirtie in a mine" (*Avarice* 1,4). *To All Angels and Saints* contrasts the seductive glitter of money with the true gold, Christ, first incarnate in the Virgin Mary. She is addressed as "the holy mine, whence came the gold,/ The great restorative for all decay" (lines 11–12). The speaker of *Deniall* asks for Christ's reincarnation in man: *"Come, come, my God, O come."* This cry from the liturgy of Advent is followed by *Christmas,* a poem in two parts. Here again, Herbert neglects the historical event in favor of its typical significance. The liturgy for Advent and Christmas distinguishes between three comings of Christ. One is His birth in Bethlehem, the second His invisible descent into the redeemed soul, and the third is His final coming on the Day of Judgment.[5] Omitting the historical birth, the first part or sonnet of *Christmas* is a prayer for Christ's indwelling in the soul; the song, the second part, looks forward to Christ's eternal day, which will begin at His last coming. The poem that concludes Herbert's reflection on the Incarnation is *Coloss. 3.3.* The motto that runs diagonally through its ten lines returns to the subject of *Avarice,* which ended: "Man calleth thee his wealth, who made thee rich;/

And while he digs out thee, falls in the ditch." In contrast, the motto of *Coloss. 3.3* declares that Christ gives a true but hidden wealth, for *"My life is hid in Him, that is my treasure."*

In the light of Herbert's almost incredible subtlety, it is danger-ous for a reader even to attempt to draw a blueprint of the antitypical design of *The Temple.* However, Herbert appears to distinguish between theory and practice: The poems before *Coloss. 3.3* lay the foundations of the doctrine of redemption and the mysteries of faith; after *Coloss. 3.3,* the emphasis is on the diffi-culties the Christian encounters in building on these foundations, in following the plan set out by the divine Architect for His temple in man's soul.

## Milton's inward temple

Of Man's First Disobedience, and the Fruit
Of that Forbidden Tree, whose mortal tast
Brought Death into the World, and all our woe,
With loss of *Eden,* till one greater Man
Restore us, and regain the blissful Seat,
Sing, Heav'nly Muse, that on the secret top
Of *Oreb,* or of *Sinai,* didst inspire
That Shepherd, who first taught the chosen Seed,
In the Beginning how the Heav'ns and Earth
Rose out of Chaos: Or if *Sion* Hill
Delight thee more, and *Siloa*'s brook that flow'd
Fast by the Oracle of God; I thence
Invoke thy aid to my adventrous Song,
That with no middle flight intends to soar
Above th' *Aonian* Mount, while it pursues
Things unattempted yet in Prose or Rime.
And chiefly Thou O Spirit, that dost prefer
Before all Temples th' upright heart and pure,
Instruct me, for Thou know'st; Thou from the first
Wast present, and with mighty wings outspread
Dove-like satst brooding on the vast Abyss
And mad'st it pregnant: What in me is dark
Illumin, what is low raise and support;
That to the highth of this great Argument
I may assert Eternal Providence,
And justifie the wayes of God to men.

*Paradise Lost,* I, 1–26

The invocation of *Paradise Lost* makes explicit use of types.[6] Adam foreshadows the greater Man, Christ, who regains Eden, "the blissful Seat." Although Christ did not relocate mankind in the original Garden of Eden, Milton's lines clearly identify Christ's restoration with man's return to paradise, and the only logical conclusion we can draw from the equation is that Eden serves for the poet as the type of man's ideal relationship with God. As type, paradise is inferior to its antitype: If Christ is the greater Man, the original Garden is the habitat of a smaller man, a place of external amenities, which become superfluous in Christ's "blissful seat." The latter is the world of grace which man may possess forever in heaven, but which he can also make his own on earth. Once Adam understands God's redemptive history and adds "Deeds to thy knowledge answerable," the loss of his local Eden no longer matters, because he will "posses/ A Paradise within thee, *happier farr*" (XII, 586–587). The "paradise within" is Eden's antitype.

The poets of antiquity invoked the Muses, who haunted the Aonian Mount, Parnassus, from which flowed the waters of the Pierian Spring, symbolizing poetic inspiration. Milton, who intends to wing higher than Parnassus, clarifies that the Christian tradition has its mountains and its waters, too. He invokes the heavenly Muse, whether she be on Oreb, Sinai, Sion's hill, or in the waters of Siloa near the Temple of Jerusalem. Yet these are not names of myth or legend, but historical places, recorded in Scripture because God addressed Himself there to man.

Milton has a reason for being so casual about the location of his Muse. God spoke occasionally in the Old Testament from external places of His choosing and gave only a partial revelation of His design. The Old Testament is part of the heritage upon which a Christian poet can draw, but it has also been complemented by God's full revelation in the New Testament. Therefore the request for assistance is particularized in:

> And chiefly Thou O Spirit, that dost prefer
> Before all Temples th' upright heart and pure,
> Instruct me, for Thou know'st . . . .

It no longer matters where the heavenly Muse used to reside in the past: the heart, the temple of the New Dispensation, replaces all earlier sacred locations, both Judaic and pagan, as the Spirit of God gives to the Christian poet an understanding that could not be conferred by the Muses of antiquity, and was delivered only in shadows and figures to the divinely inspired writers of the Old Testament. Several architectural metaphors are submerged in lines 17–24. The poet asks that his heart be made an "upright" or 'vertical' temple of grand proportions, girded by the Spirit, who must "raise" and "support" its "low" roof in order that this epic may be built to correspond to the "highth" of God's architecture of history.

The acceptance of biblical types follows upon the belief that God guides the world. All of history is *gesta dei,* a record of divine accomplishment, and every detail in it is part of His pattern. The latter must include pagan antiquity, its mythology, ethics and religion, because nothing, past or present, occurs without God's will or sufferance. Therefore, three levels of comparison exist in Milton's opening discourse. It clearly differentiates between the Old and the New Dispensation, but both of these are contrasted with pagan antiquity, which is recalled for the reader by the genre, the style, and the references to Muse, mountains, and waters. The pagan world, too, is a world of types, but with an important difference: Paganism is the result of Satan's perversion of God's plan.

Satan always borrows God's patterns; he never discovers a method of his own, but merely abuses whatever he can see of God's mode of operation. When he begins his rebellion in heaven, he calls his legions to "his royal seat," The Palace of Great Lucifer, which

> . . . not long after, he
> Affecting all equality with God,
> In imitation of that Mount whereon
> *Messiah* was declar'd in sight of Heav'n,
> The Mountain of the Congregation called;
> V, 762–766

Sion, meaning "lifted up," was the mountain on which the Israelites gathered; it foreshadowed the Christian Church, or *Ecclesia,* which means "congregation." Both Sion and *Ecclesia* prefigure for man their eternal antitypes, the final gathering of the elect on God's Mount of Congregation in heaven. The proud Lucifer therefore starts with a cheap, distorted imitation of God's order in heaven. And later, in hell, Satan must, like God, have his own palace and place of worship, the Pandemonium of Book I. It is "Built like a Temple" (713) and stands, of course, on a hill (670), with artificial lights copied after the blazing stars of God's empyrean:

> . . . from the arched roof
> Pendant by subtle Magic many a row
> Of Starry Lamps and blazing Cressets fed
> With *Naphtha* and *Asphaltus* yeilded light
> As from a sky.
>
> 726–730

After God sets out the order of His worship for the children of Israel, the devils take on new names and try to invade His sacred precincts. Moloch made Solomon "build/ His temple right against the Temple of God" (I, 401–402); Astarte was known in Sion "where stood/ Her Temple on th' offensive Mountain" (I, 442–443); Thammuz was worshipped "in the sacred Porch" of the Temple of Jerusalem with a display of "wanton passions" by the daughters of Sion (I, 446–455); Dagon was "dreaded through the Coast/ Of *Palestine*" (I, 464–465), and Rimmon "also against the house of God was bold" (I, 470). Simultaneously the devils move beyond Palestine to spread false religion among the Gentiles. Again they use for their perverse activity the method of God; they work with His types: temples and mountains. Thus, through Satan's efforts, the pagan world becomes the shadow of God's design. Milton's belief in divine types and in Satan's perversion of them allows him to incorporate into his Christian epic so many allusions to pagan myth and history. He sees a similarity of pattern everywhere; only the details and the names vary.

The Satanic obsession with outward temples, which Milton repeatedly stresses in Book I, is in ironic contrast to the poet's opening statement that God's preferred temple is that of the pure and upright heart. Satan and his host see God's method but have no knowledge of His purpose. They observe His types but do not know that these are only His foreshadowings. They mistake a type or figure for His reality, which they are driven to destroy. Hence, their continual frustration; they believe that by destroying the

Garden they can ruin forever the bond between God and man, and that by claiming possession of mountains and temples they can abolish the worship of God. In fact, however, they merely aid God in the fulfillment of His design: they are instrumental in bringing about the antitypical inward temple and the paradise within.

Milton's typology is not identical with that of Herbert. Although they both derive their types from Scripture, they differ in the application of them. Herbert's interpretation is reminiscent of the Epistle to the Hebrews, in which Old Testament types prefigure the antitypes of the New, and both in turn anticipate the full revelation of heaven. Herbert's Church of England, with its priesthood, liturgy, and obedience to a temporal king, is a halfway point. Behind it lie the figures of the ineffectual temple, priesthood, and kingship of the Hebrew past; before it is the communion of saints in Christ's eternal priesthood and kingship in heaven. Herbert and his companions on the Anglican *via media* were content to live under king and bishop, and they revered these offices as part of God's design and as reflections of His invisible power and glory.

Milton's approach, on the other hand, usually recalls that of Paul: The New Dispensation has abrogated the claims of the Old. Christ's Redemption is for Milton also a revolution that has transformed the world. When the Hebrews lived under the law, their priesthood and kingship were necessary institutions to guide a blind and weak people. But if the Redemption is revolutionary, priesthood and kingship are superfluous. Through faith in Christ and the working of His grace, every man is his own king and priest: "we now under Christ, a royal priesthood, I *Pet.* 2.9, as we are coheirs, kings and priests with him . . . ." [7] No power, civil or ecclesiastical, has absolute claim on the Christian's allegiance:

> All Protestants hold that Christ in his church hath left no vicegerent of his power, but himself without deputie, is the only head thereof, governing it from heaven: how then can any Christian-man derive his kingship from Christ, but with wors usurpation than the Pope his headship over the church, since Christ not only hath not left the least shaddow of a command for any such vice-gerence from him in the State, as the Pope pretends for his in the Church, but hath expressly declar'd, that such regal dominion is from the gentiles, not from him, and hath strictly charg'd us, not to imitate them therin. [8]

## Vaughan: "Isaacs Marriage"

Vaughan's frequent borrowings of Herbert's phrases and lines prove that he is a disciple of the older poet, but he is more than Herbert's fading echo.[9] The title of his most memorable volume, *Silex Scintillans* (*The Sparkling Flint*), does not imply the careful ordering of poems in the manner of *The Temple;* it promises only moments of illumination. And yet the lights struck from the flint do combine into constellations: Many of Vaughan's poems form sequences through correspondence or contrast, imagery, and diction. It would take another book to illustrate this practice, but a diligent reader can discover for himself that, for example, the first ten poems of *Silex Scintillans* are interwoven with images of wells, springs, and fountains, of gardens, flowers, and spices, of light, gold, and vital rays, of weddings, bride, and bridegroom. Moreover, the theme of one poem leads logically to that of the next. "Regeneration" concludes *let me dye before my death!"* and is followed by "Death," a dialogue between body and soul. The soul assures the body that the grave will merely be a temporary residence and that their union will be restored on the morning of the everlasting day: "Then shall wee meet to mixe again." The dialogue is continued in "Resurrection and Immortality." This poem offers proof of the belief that "no thing can to *Nothing* fall" in the example of the silkworm, which escapes "its silent cell" after a "long sleepe" and wings away; so body and soul will be "Both wing'd and free" at the end of days, but between now and that glorious future stands the event of the next poem, "Day of Judgement." Man must prepare himself to appear before the tribunal of the just God with "A living *FAITH*, a *HEART* of flesh/ The *WORLD* an Enemie"; that is to say, the soul cannot hope for salvation without a religious life. "Religion," which follows, complains that Christ's well of living water has become "a tainted sink." The hope of "Regeneration" has reached an impasse; Christ has passed from the world. Hence, "The Search" describes the "roving Extasie/ To find my Saviour." The speaker returns to the places of the Saviour's life, Bethlehem, Egypt, the Temple of Jerusalem, Jacob's well at Sychar, the garden of the Agony, the hill of the Crucifixion, and Christ's empty grave. All his roving is fruitless, and he decides that Christ must be in His preferred place of solitude, the wilderness. The speaker naively anticipates that the presence of God will have transformed the desert into a garden of delights. The searching is in vain for the reason that the speaker looks for physical evidence and outward signs. But God resides no longer in the typical places of His grace; the temple is "A little dust," and Jacob's well an "angry Spring." The types have been discarded, because the promise implied in them has been fulfilled. A singing voice instructs the searcher:

> Leave, leave, thy gadding thoughts;
>> Who Pores
>> and spies
> Still out of Doores
>> descries
> Within them nought.

> . . . . . . .

> Search well another world; who studies this,
> Travels in Clouds, seeks *Manna,* where none is.

The only *Manna* the speaker may hope to find is Christ's grace within his soul. Appended to "The Search" is a quotation from Acts (17:27–28): "That they should seek the Lord, if happily they might feel after him, and finde him, though he be not far off from every one of us, for in him we live, and move, and have our being."

The error in "The Search" is the misreading of types; in contrast, "*Isaacs* Marriage" offers a lesson in right reading. In the history of typology Isaac is an important figure of Christ. The sacrifice of his life, narrowly averted by an intervening angel in Genesis 22, foreshadowed the Saviour's death. Augustine, in his *Tractate on the Gospel of John,* points out that "Isaac bore the wood for his offering, Christ his cross."[10] Chrysostom, in *The Fourth Homily on II Corinthians,* comments on Isaac's *typical* meekness: "For of Him [Christ] he both imitated the gentleness, and kept to the type. For *he was led like a lamb to the slaughter, and as a sheep dumb before his shearer* (Isa. 4:7)."[11] Luther finds a typological reason for the timely substitution of a ram for Isaac: "The hidden sense is that just as Isaac was led away to be sacrificed but in the end was saved and a ram caught in the thorns was sacrificed in his stead, so the Son of God, since he was both mortal and immortal in one and the same person, was sacrificed, but only his flesh, that is his humanity, was slain."[19]

Vaughan comments on the effect of Isaac's sacrifice:

> But thou a Chosen sacrifice wert given,
> And offer'd up so early unto heaven
> Thy flames could not be out; Religion was
> Ray'd into thee, like beams into a glasse,
> Where, as thou grewst, it multipli'd and shin'd
> The sacred Constellation of thy mind.

Isaac, like Abraham, was righteous through faith and thus a type of the New Testament followers of Christ. The first twenty-nine lines of *"Isaacs* Marriage" recapitulate the theme of "Religion," the contrast between the "White dayes" of God's early converse with man and the decayed, poisoned religion of the present—there are no Christians who fulfill the promise represented by Abraham and his son.

The marriage of Isaac is also a traditional type. The servant sent by Abraham to arrange the marriage met Rebekah at the well of Nahor. He brought her back to his master's country, and Isaac, who had gone to meet his future wife, greeted her at the well of Lahairoi. A passage from Gregory of Nyssa's sermon on the baptism of Christ illuminates the *typical* meaning of the fountains, springs, and wells in *Silex Scintillans:*

> Behold then, a sacramental type: how from the very first it is by the means of living water that salvation comes to him that was perishing . . . . Abraham's servant is sent to make the match, so as to secure a bride for his master, and finds Rebekah at the well: and a marriage that was to produce the race of Christ had its beginning and its first covenant in water. Yes, and Isaac himself also, when he was ruling his flocks, digged wells, in all parts of the desert, which the aliens stopped and filled up, for a type of all those who hindered the grace of Baptism, and talked loudly in their struggle against the truth.[13]

As Isaac, digger of wells, foreshadows Christ's release of the life-giving water of baptism, so does his bride prefigure the bride of Christ, the Church. Rebekah dispenses the water from the well, as the Church channels the grace of baptism to all who wish to follow Christ. The chaste simplicity of Rebekah's appearance and conduct (lines 31–42) is the ideal that the Church ought to embody.

The comparison of Isaac's prayer to the transformation of water into cloud, and of cloud into rain falling on "the thirstie Isle" (lines 53–62), is an allegory of the sacrifice of Christ, Whose blood, offered up to Heaven, returns to man as life-giving water. It also echoes the lesson of "Ressurrection and Immortality":

> For no thing can to *Nothing* fall, but still
>     Incorporates by skill,
> And then returns, and from the wombe of things
>     Such treasure brings
>     As *Phenix*-like renew'th
>     Both life, and youth.

The conclusion that Isaac is a "young Patriarch" and a "marri'd Saint" is not paradoxical if we apply it to Isaac's antitype. Christ never attained on earth the ripe age of the Old Testament patriarchs, but He is the spiritual patriarch, the giver of eternal life, to all those who believe in Him. He was the saintliest of men, mysteriously conceived, born from a virgin, and untainted by the weakness of the flesh; yet He married: He entered into a marriage with His bride, the Church.

"The Brittish Church" describes what has happened to the bride. She lives in *mists* and *shadows* of false religion, divided by strife and dissension. Instead of the beauty of Rebekah, she has but "ravished looks/ Slain flock, and pillaged fleeces." Vaughan's indictment of the decay of religion in his age is severe. The marriage of Isaac was meant by God as a figure of a more glorious and substantial reality. The intended antitype, the fulfillment of that union, is Christ's life in the Church. The bride has been so corrupted, however, that Christ has fled from her, and she no longer bears any resemblance to her type, Rebekah. God's plan has been reversed: The type now appears more glorious than the antitype.

The examples of typological usage in Herbert, Milton, and Vaughan should make it clear that in order to understand the greater portion of seventeenth-century literature there is no substitute for a knowledge of Scripture. The writers constantly drew on the Bible for their diction and imagery. From Donne to Milton, most English authors understood man, the world, and the history of both in the light of Scripture. Their interpretations varied in style, in ingenuity, and in the conclusions, but their perspective and method were remarkably similar and typical.

# Conclusion

Emerson declared that "a fact is the end or last issue of spirit," but he went on to say that "this doctrine is abstruse." For him the relation between mind and matter was like "the Sphinx at the roadside, and from age to age, as each prophet comes by, he tries his fortune at reading her riddle." Here lies the radical difference between the romantic mind and that of the generations of Donne and Milton. Emerson admired individual and original speculation about the realm of the spirit; the early seventeenth century still accepted an inherited, communal, and Christian interpretation of the transcendental world. Men of that age derived their spirituality from the Bible, and the prophets of other ages were carefully evaluated; the status of prophets was determined by their approximation to divinely revealed truth.

The age admired primarily, not originality of ideas, but virtuosity in the manipulation of known materials. Since the Renaissance, the stock and store of knowledge had been marvelously multiplied. The humanists introduced a new study of history and the thoughts and arts of ancient generations. Travel and improved communications increased men's awareness of their present moment. In the years between the death of Elizabeth I and the accession of Charles II, the variety of this newly found knowledge begins dangerously to strain the bounds of the old world picture. Yet the rupture does not occur till later; for Donne and Milton, circle and center still hold. The literary minds of the age attempt to bring vagabond details under control; they must order things so that they can master them. They then delight in showing this mastery in their ability to manipulate with astonishing ingenuity all that they have learned in history and science, in theology and philosophy, in classical and Christian thought, and in literary conventions and traditions. *Paradise Lost* is indisputably the greatest work of the age. It is a visionary poem, but its vision is not intuitive; rather, it is the result of a grandiose synthesis by a virtuoso among virtuosi.

# Notes

## Notes to Chapter One

1. A. S. P. Woodhouse, *Puritanism and Liberty* (London, 1938), pp. 63–4, 83.

2. Nowell's *Catechism* is the subject of a separate chapter; for bibliographical details see the text of Ch. V, Section 1, and the corresponding notes.

3. Quotations from Herrick follow the text of *The Complete Poetry of Robert Herrick*, J. Max Patrick, ed. (New York, 1963). Paul O. Clark contends that "The Hock-Cart" gives no evidence of capitalist exploitation—see his article in *Explicator*, XXIV (1966), item 70. The first full-length critical study of Herrick is Roger B. Rollin's *Robert Herrick* (New York, 1966).

4. W. K. Jordan arrives at the figure 4,400 on the basis of a statistical survey of London and ten counties in *Philanthropy in England, 1480–1660* (London, 1959), pp. 279–97. The second figure is mentioned by M. H. Curtis in "Education and Apprenticeship," *Shakespeare in His Own Age,* Allardyce Nicoll, ed. (Cambridge, 1964), p. 58.

5. W. K. Jordan, pp. 152–239.

6. *Ibid.,* pp. 317–18. For a survey of the economic and political changes on the lowest level of the Church of England see Christopher Hill, "The Secularization of the Parish," *Society and Puritanism in Pre-Revolutionary England* (New York, 1967), pp. 420–42.

7. W. K. Jordan, p. 294, and Lawrence Stone, *The Crisis of the Aristocracy, 1558–1641* (Oxford, 1965), p. 688.

8. This thesis is propounded by M. H. Curtis, "The Alienated Intellectuals of Early Stuart England," *Past and Present,* No. 23 (1962), reprinted in *Crisis in Europe,* Trevor Aston, ed. (London, 1965), pp. 309–331. Although Curtis does not mention Burton, the historian's facts and figures support the complaints and allegations in the "Digression on the Misery of Scholars." Quotations from Burton's *The Anatomy of Melancholy* are taken from the edition by Lawrence Babb (Lansing, Mich., 1965). Babb's edition is not complete but offers a judicious selection; excluded are the parts that deal with anatomy, diet, and pharmacology; all of Burton's Latin quotations are supplied with English versions.

9. M. H. Curtis, in "The Alienated Intellectuals . . . ," n. 24, mentions Lord William Russell's attempt to invalidate the will of his wife on the grounds that the portions she left to some 'trencher chaplains' were too large.

10. Fifteen to twenty is the "probable" percentage arrived at by M. H. Curtis in "The Alienated Intellectuals . . . ," *Crisis in Europe,* p. 331.

11. *Ibid.,* p. 319, and W. K. Jordan, p. 291.

12. For details on the system of apprenticeship see: C. R. B. Barrett, *The History of the Society of Apothecaries of London* (London, 1905); M. G. Davies, *The Enforcement of English Apprenticeship* (Cambridge, Mass., 1956); Douglas Knoop and G. P. Jones, *The London Mason in the Seventeenth Century* (Manchester, 1935); D. F. McKenzie, *Stationers' Company Apprentice 1605–1640* (Charlottesville, Va., 1961).

13. G. P. V. Akrigg, *Jacobean Pageant* (Cambridge, Mass. 1963), pp. 31–32.

14. The title page of the first edition has: "Written about Twenty three yeares ago, for the Benefit of *Rotherham* School, where it was first used, and after 14. years trial by diligent practise in *London* in many particulars enlarged, and now at last published for the general profit, especially of young Schoole-Masters." Quotations from *A New Discovery* . . . are from the

edition by E. T. Campagnac (Liverpool and London, 1913). Hoole gives a rather cryptic list of the "Schoole-Authours, most proper for every Form of Scholars in a Grammar-Schoole"—the most accurate seventeenth-century bibliography of textbooks that we know of. Nearly all the titles briefly referred to in Hoole's list have been identified by Foster Watson in *A Bibliographical Account of Education in England, 1500–1660* (U.S. Bureau of Education, 1903). Milton's education has been reconstructed in detail by Donald L. Clark, *John Milton at St. Paul's School* (New York, 1948), and by Harris F. Fletcher, *The Intellectual Development of John Milton*, 2 vols. (Urbana, Ill., 1956). St. Paul's was one of the finest schools in England, so that Milton's education is likely to have been exceptional. I have restricted myself to rendering Hoole's program, because it appears to be based on broad experience in and outside London.

15. In the remainder of this section the references to the average ages of pupils of various levels of their education will apply to city children only; the reader must keep in mind that pupils living in the countryside were usually 'retarded' by a few years.

16. *The Diary of Samuel Pepys*, H. B. Wheatley, ed. (London, 1893–1899), II, 259.

17. Unless otherwise indicated, the critical pronouncements of Jonson quoted in this book are from the selections of *Timber: or, Disoveries*, newly edited by E. W. Tayler in his anthology *Literary Criticism of Seventeenth-Century England* (New York, 1967). Tayler's introduction is a brief and excellent survey of the critical assumptions of the period, and his bibliography is useful.

18. *Opera Omnia* (Leyden, 1703), I, 3. (translation by the present author).

19. *Of Education*, Thomas R. Hartmann, ed., in *The Prose of John Milton*, J. Max Patrick, general ed. (New York, 1968), p. 232. Unless otherwise noted, all quotations from Milton's prose will be to this edition of significant selections, hereafter referred to as *Prose*, Patrick. The full text of Milton's prose is only available in the Columbia University edition of the complete works in 18 volumes (1931–38); a new edition by the Yale University Press of the complete prose with historical introductions and copious notes is still in progress; four out of eight projected volumes have thus far appeared in print.

20. *Familiaria Colloquia;* the probable date of the first edition is 1533.

21. For a survey of the Renaissance passion for division and subdivision in rhetoric, see Sister Miriam Joseph, C.S.C., *Shakespeare's Use of the Arts of Language* (New York, 1947), pp. 31–39.

22. DeWitt T. Starnes and E. W. Talbert, *Classical Myth and Legend in Renaissance Dictionaries* (Chapel Hill, N.C., 1955), pp. 3–10.

23. For extensive documentation of Jonson's and Milton's debt to the dictionaries, see Chs. VI and VIII in Starnes and Talbert.

24. Harris F. Fletcher, II, 293, 297.

25. L. H. D. Buxton and S. Gibson, *Oxford University Ceremonies* (Oxford, 1935), pp. 1–2.

26. The information concerning the requirements for the B.A. and M.A. degrees at Oxford has been abstracted from Buxton and Gibson, pp. 1–10, and 67–72.

27. Graduate study was divided between the faculties of theology, medicine, law, and music. The first of these was still the most flourishing in Milton's time. The faculty of law grew increasingly less significant. Before the Reformation the universities had lectured on civil and canon law, both of which derived their concept of the rule of law from the Roman legal system. Henry VIII, sorely frustrated in his first divorce proceedings by the canon law of the Papal Curia, abolished its teaching in England. Also, during the sixteenth century common law came to prevail over the still inadequate code of civil law. To train in common law, one went to the Inns of Court in London, so the legal minds at the universities were left with few cases for debate and judgment. The study of medicine at Oxford and Cambridge lagged far behind the advances made at such famous continental centers as Montpellier, Padua, and Leyden. See W. T. Costello, S. J., *The Scholastic Curriculum at Early Seventeenth-Century Cambridge* (Cambridge, Mass., 1958), pp. 107–141, and Phyllis Allen, "Medical Education in 17th-Century England," *Journal of the History of Medicine*, I (1946), 115–43.

28. W. T. Costello, pp. 11–14.

29. M. H. Curtis, *Oxford and Cambridge in Transition, 1558–1642* (Oxford, 1959), Chs. IV and V.

30. M. H. Curtis, "The Alienated Intellectuals . . . ," *Crisis in Europe,* p. 320.

31. Buxton and Gibson, pp. 84–85; Stone, pp. 688–690.

32. My synopsis of the method of instruction is derived from W. T. Costello, pp. 41–46, and *passim.*

33. *Ibid.,* p. 10.

34. Sister Miriam Joseph, pp. 18–23.

35. The indisputable authority on Ramism is Walter J. Ong, S. J., especially in his *Ramus: Method, and the Decay of Dialogue* (Cambridge, Mass., 1958). Rosemond Tuve's difficult *Elizabethan and Metaphysical Imagery* (Chicago, 1961) attributes the logical exactness of the metaphysicals to Ramist influence. Her thesis has been assailed by N. E. Nelson, "Peter Ramus and the Confusion of Logic, Rhetoric and Poetry," *University of Michigan Contributions in Modern Philosophy,* II (1947), 1–22, and by A. J. Smith, "An Examination of Some Claims for Ramism," *Review of English Studies,* VII (1956), 349–59. For a brief survey and evaluation of Ramus, Ramism, and the controversy, see K. G. Hamilton, *The Two Harmonies; Poetry and Prose in the Seventeenth Century* (Oxford, 1963), pp. 107–119, and Harris F. Fletcher, II, 142–146. See also Peter F. Fisher, "Milton's Logic," *Journal of the History of Ideas,* XXIII (1962), 37–60, and John M. Major, "Milton's View of Rhetoric," *Studies in Philology,* LXIV (1967), 685–701.

36. All quotations from Milton's poems follow the text established by John T. Shawcross in *The Complete English Poetry of John Milton* (New York, 1963).

37. *Selected Writings of Francis Bacon,* with an introduction and notes by Hugh G. Dick (New York, 1955), p. 243.

38. *Ibid.,* pp. 245, 247.

39. *Of Education, Prose,* Patrick, p. 236.

40. *De augmentis scientiarum, the Works of Sir Francis Bacon,* James Spedding, R. L. Ellis, and D. D. Heath, eds., 7 vols. (London, 1879), IV, 455.

41. *Ibid.,* p. 456.

42. *Selected Writings,* Dick, p. 245.

43. *The Reason of Church-Government,* E. H. Emerson, ed., *Prose,* Patrick, pp. 109–110.

44. Quotations from Herbert follow the text of F. E. Hutchinson, *The Works of George Herbert* (Oxford, 1941). Quotations from Vaughan follow the text of French Fogle, *The Complete Poetry of Henry Vaughan* (New York, 1965).

45. *Ben Jonson,* C. H. Herford and P. Simpson, eds., 11 vols. (Oxford, 1925–52), VIII, 636.

46. *The Reason of Church-Government, Prose,* Patrick, p. 107.

47. *An Apology Against a Pamphlet . . . ,* Emerson, ed., *Prose,* Patrick, p. 117.

48. Preface to the second edition of *Silex Scintillans,* Fogle, p. 260.

49. See *The Defenses,* John R. Mulder, ed. and trans., *Prose,* Patrick, p. 417.

50. Quotations from the *Religio Medici* follow the text edited by Jean-Jacques Denonain (Cambridge, 1953); the complete edition of Browne's *Works* is by G. Keynes, 4 vols. (Chicago, 1964); a carefully edited, very generous selection is *The Prose of Sir Thomas Browne,* N.J. Endicott, ed. (New York, 1967).

51. See Thomas Kranidas, "Milton and the Rhetoric of Zeal," *Texas Studies in Language and Literature,* VI (1965), 423–432, and, by the same author, "Decorum and the Style of Milton's Antiprelatical Tracts," *Studies in Philology,* LXII (1965), 155–175. Kranidas has analyzed

Milton's concept of decorum and its importance in the critical evaluation of the pamphlets and of *Paradise Lost* in *The Fierce Equation* (The Hague, 1965).

## Notes to Chapter Two

1. Quotations from Donne's poetry follow the text of the edition by John T. Shawcross, *The Complete Poetry of John Donne* (New York, 1968). Helen Gardner's edition, *The Elegies and the Songs and Sonnets of John Donne* (New York, 1965) has an excellent commentary. The elegies have recently been discussed by N. J. C. Andreasen in *John Donne: Conservative Revolutionary* (Princeton, 1967). Joan Webber has shed much light on Donne's use of logic and rhetoric in *Contrary Music: The Prose Style of John Donne* (Madison, 1963).

2. Dudley Fenner, *The Artes of Logike* and *Rethorike* (Middleburg, 1584), Sig. B4$^v$.

3. Raphe Lever, *The Arte of Reason, Rightly Termed Witcraft* (London, 1573), p. 174.

4. D. Fenner, Sig. B2.

5. W. T. Costello, pp. 14–19.

6. The list of topics is a selection from a lengthier one culled from students' notebooks by W. T. Costello, pp. 58–59.

7. *De Aug., Works,* IV, 456.

8. The most elaborate analysis of "The Canonization," as well as of five other poems by Donne, is by Clay Hunt in his *Donne's Poetry* (New Haven, 1954). For stimulating insights see also Arnold Stein's difficult book, *John Donne's Lyrics: The Eloquence of Action* (Minneapolis, 1962). Setting previous critics on their heads, John Guss demonstrates that Donne follows the Petrarchan tradition instead of opposing it; see his *John Donne, Petrarchist* (Detroit, 1966).

9. Quotations from Marvell's poems follow the text as edited by George de F. Lord in Andrew Marvell, *Complete Poetry* (New York, 1968). See Joan Hartwig, "The Principle of Measure in 'To His Coy Mistress,'" *College English,* XXV (1964), 572–575.

10. As does one of Marvell's recent critics, J. B. Leishman, in *The Art of Marvell's Poetry* (London, 1966), p. 38.

11. For a survey of the history of the interpretation of the *Anniversaries,* see Frank Manley's introduction to his edition of the two poems (Baltimore, 1963), pp. 1–61. Huntley's analysis of *Urne-Buriall* and *The Garden of Cyrus* is part of his *Sir Thomas Browne: A Biographical and Critical Study* (Ann Arbor, Mich., 1963), pp. 204–223. Other recent works on Browne are Joan Bennett's *Sir Thomas Browne* (New York, 1962) and Robert R. Cawley and George Yost's *Studies in Sir Thomas Browne* (Eugene, Or., 1965); see also Leonard Nathanson, *The Strategy of Truth* (Chicago, 1967).

12. See Stella Revard, "Milton's Critique of Heroic Warfare in *Paradise Lost* V and VI," *Studies in English Literature,* VII (1967), 119–139. For a close reading of the Battle in Heaven— and other important scenes of *Paradise Lost*—see also Stanley E. Fish, *Surprised by Sin* (New York, 1967). On Milton's adaptation of traditions see John M. Steadman, *Milton and the Renaissance Hero* (New York, 1967) and Davis P. Harding, *The Club of Hercules: Studies in the Classical Background of Paradise Lost* (Urbana, 1962). On the structure of Milton's epic see especially Isabel MacCaffrey's *Paradise Lost as 'Myth'* (Cambridge, Mass., 1959) and J. R. Watson's "Divine Providence and the Structure of Paradise Lost," *Essays in Criticism,* XIV (1964), 148–155.

13. *The Second Defense . . . , Prose,* Patrick, p. 411.

14. In the famous portrait of Cromwell in *The Second Defense (Prose,* Patrick, pp. 422–428) and in Sonnet 16, *"Cromwell,* our cheif of men . . . ."

15. Browne always italicizes proper names and foreign words; all other italics in the quotations from *Religio Medici* are mine.

16. According to a very ancient belief, Hermes was an Egyptian prophet contemporary with Moses, and his philosophy was thought to have influenced Pythagoras and Plato. Hermetism was a subject of special interest during the Renaissance, the Florentine neo-Platonists having

had a predilection for the hieratic Hermetic stance. See Frances A. Yates, *Giordano Bruno and the Hermetic Tradition* (Chicago, 1964).

17. J. B. Bamborough, *The Little World of Man* (London, 1952), pp. 30, 83. See also C. A. Patrides, "The Microcosm of Man: Further References to a Commonplace," *Notes & Queries*, X (1963), 282–286.

## Notes to Chapter Three

1. Sir Thomas Browne, *Pseudodoxia Epidemica*, Bk. I, Ch. 4, Endicott, ed., p. 114.

2. Recent discussions of this poem are A. E. Berthoff's "The Allegorical Metaphor: Marvell's 'Definition of Love'," *Review of English Studies*, VVII (1966), 16–24; E. J. Schulze's "The Reach of Witt: Marvell's 'The Definition of Love'," *Papers of the Michigan Academy*, L (1955), 563–574; H. E. Toliver's "Marvell's 'The Definition of Love'," *Bucknell Review*, X (1965), 263–274; and a note by Laurie Zwickie in *Explicator*, XXII (1964), item 52. See also the full-length critical study by L. W. Hyman, *Andrew Marvell* (New York, 1964).

3. Mary Ellen Rickey comments extensively on Herbert's talent for punning, in *Utmost Art: Complexity in the Verse of George Herbert* (Lexington, Ky., 1966).

4. See Bernard Knieger, "The Purchase-Sale: Patterns of Business Imagery in the Poetry of George Herbert," *Studies in English Literature*, VI (1966), 111–124.

5. Joseph Spence, *Anecdotes*, J. M. Osborne, ed. (Oxford, 1966), I, 434.

6. *The Reason of Church-Government . . . , Prose*, Patrick, p. 107.

7. The following authors have recently commented on aspects of Milton's style: Lewis H. Fenderson, "The Onomato-Musical Element in *Paradise Lost*," *College Language Association Journal*, IX (1966), 255–264; Anne Davidson Ferry, *Milton's Epic Voice: The Narrator in Paradise Lost* (Cambridge, Mass. 1963); Joseph Frank, "The Unharmonious Vision: Milton as Baroque Artist," *Comparative Literature Studies*, III (1966), 95–108; Christopher Grose, "Some Uses of Sensuous Immediacy in *Paradise Lost*," *Huntington Library Quarterly*, XXXI (1968), 211–222; Douglas Knight, "The Dramatic Center of *Paradise Lost*," *South Atlantic Quarterly*, LXIII (1964), 44–59; Harold E. Toliver, "Complicity of Voice in *Paradise Lost*," *Modern Language Quarterly*, XXV (1964), 153–170; Thomas Wheeler, "Milton's Blank Verse Couplets," *Journal of English and Germanic Philology*, LXVI (1967), 359–368; Michael Wilding, "*Paradise Lost* and Linguistic Precision," *Balcony*, No. 5 (1966), 25–31. The most lucid study is Christopher Ricks's *Milton's Grand Style* (New York, 1963).

## Notes to Chapter Four

1. *The Life and Times of Anthony à Wood*, abridged from Andrew Clark's edn. in 5 vols. (1891–1900), with an introduction by Llewelyn Powys (London, 1961), p. 33.

2. *On Christian Doctrine*, trans. by D. W. Robertson (New York, 1958), p. 122.

3. *The Autobiography and Correspondence of Sir Simonds D'Ewes, Bart*, James O Halliwell, ed., 2 vols. (London, 1845), I, 120.

4. *Memoirs of the Verney Family*, III, 74; cited from Maurice Ashley, *The Stuarts in Love* (New York, 1963), p. 8.

5. *History and Antiquities of the University of Oxford*, J. Gutch, ed., 2 vols. (London, 1792–6), II, 653.

6. Buxton and Gibson, pp. 106–7.

7. F. L. Huntley, p. 37.

8. W. J. Costello, p. 110.

9. See Foster Watson, "Scholars and Scholarship, 1600–60," *Cambridge History of English Literature*, VII, 304–24.

10. Christopher Hill, "The Ratsbane of Lecturing," *Society and Puritanism*, pp. 79–123.

11. Cited from Mary Coate, *Social Life in Stuart England* (London, 1924), p. 56.

12. *Life and Times,* Powys, p. 55.

13. *Ibid.,* p. 103.

14. *Ibid.,* pp. 104–5.

15. G. P. V. Akrigg, pp. 308–311.

16. Cited from John Tulloch, *Rational Theology and Christian Philosophy in England in the 17th Century,* 2 vols. (London, 1874; reprinted at Hildesheim, 1966), I, 44.

17. The summary of Arminian doctrine is an extract from Tulloch, I, 14–36.

18. For biographical sketches of the Falkland circle see Douglas Bush, *English Literature in the Earlier Seventeenth Century* (New York, 1952, 1964), pp. 324–7.

19. *Works* (Oxford, 1838), I, 404.

20. For the history of Little Gidding see B. Blackstone's *The Ferrar Papers* (1938) and A. L. Maycock's *Nicholas Ferrar of Little Gidding* (1938).

21. Acts, 7:12 *ff.*

22. Rom. 1:18 *ff.*

23. Jean Daniélou, S. J. *God and the Ways of Knowing,* trans. by Walter Roberts (New York, 1957), pp. 26–27. On the popularity and significance of paradox in the Renaissance see Rosalie Colie's *Paradoxia Epidemica* (Princeton, 1966). See also John F. N. New, "Cromwell and the Paradoxes of Puritanism," *Journal of British Studies,* V (1965), 53–59.

24. Erich Przywara, *An Augustine Synthesis* (New York, 1958), p. 68.

25. *Ibid.,* p. 58.

26. *Ibid.,* p. 64.

27. Cited in Charles N. Cochrane, *Christianity and Classical Culture* (Oxford, 1939), p. 445.

## Notes to Chapter Five

1. For a biographical sketch of Nowell see G. E. Corrie's introduction to his ediction of the first Latin and English texts of *A Catechism or First Instruction and Learning of Christian Religion* (1570), *The Parker Society Publications,* XXXII (Cambridge, 1853), i–ix. Quotations from the *Catechism* follow Corrie's edition.

2. Nowell and William Day, bishop of Winchester, were the joint authors of *A true report of the disputation or rather private conference had in the Tower of London, with Ed. Campion Jesuite, the last of August. 1581. Set downe by the reverend learned men themselves that dealt therein (1581).*

3. Corrie, p. iv.

4. The letter is reprinted in Corrie's introduction, p̃. vi.

5. For the number and dates of the editions, see A. W. Pollard, G. R. Redgrave, *et al., Short-Title Catalogue of Books Printed in England, Scotland, & Ireland . . . 1475–1640* (1926) and D. Wing's addition to this work for the years 1641–1700 (New York, 1945–51).

6. Particularly Calvin, in his *Institutes,* I, xi.

7. F. E. Hutchinson, p. 255.

8. In practice Nowell felt compelled to confute Roman Catholicism on many points.

9. The two parts of Sir Thomas Browne's *Religio Medici* deal with faith and charity; although Browne does not indicate this division in subtitles, the opening of the second part makes clear that he has that distinction in mind: "Now for that other Vertue of Charity, without which Faith is a meer notion, and of no existence . . . ." In Herbert's *The Temple* the poem *Faith* is preceded by *Repentance.*

10. *De doctrina christiana, Works* (Columbia), Vol. XVI, 101.

11. The critical opinions listed in the text are, respectively, those of E. M. W. Tillyard, Edwin Greenlaw, C. S. Lewis, and Clarence C. Green; they are reviewed and rejected in the first three chapters of A. J. A. Waldock's *Paradise Lost and Its Critics* (Cambridge, 1947). Waldock himself cannot accept obedience as a definition of the Fall, and concludes that Milton was simply not competent to handle his chosen topic. More recent and reliable expositions of Milton's doctrine are by C. A. Patrides, *Milton and the Christian Tradition* (1966); H. F. Robins, *If This Be Heresy: A Study of Milton and Origen* (1963); and James H. Sims, *The Bible in Milton's Epics* (1962).

12. *Whole Works,* C. P. Eden, ed. (London, 1847–52), II, 443.

13. See a rare essay on the tone of Herrick's religious verse by Miriam K. Starkman, *"Noble Numbers* and the Poetry of Devotion," in *Reason and the Imagination,* Joseph A. Mazzeo, ed. (New York, 1962).

14. On the impersonal voice of the epic poet, see Ch. I of E. M. W. Tillyard's *The English Epic and its Background* (London, 1954).

## Notes to Chapter Six

1. My treatment of typology is merely a sketch of a difficult topic. For further clarification see the lucid exposition on each book of the New Testament in *The Cambridge Bible Commentary* (17 volumes have appeared at present); see also G. W. H. Lampe and K. J. Woollcombe, *Essays in Typology* (Naperville, Ill., 1957); J. Daniélou, S. J., *From Shadows to Reality: Studies in the Typology of the Fathers,* trans. by W. Hibberd (Westminster, Md., 1960); on the literary adaptation of typology see Erich Auerbach's "Figura," *Scenes from the Drama of European Literature* (New York, 1959), pp. 11–76.

2. Even Isaac Newton followed a typological approach to history; see Frank E. Manuel, *Isaac Newton Historian* (Cambridge, Mass., 1963).

3. For a description of Donne's exegetical method see Evelyn M. Simpson's introduction to *John Donne's Sermons on the Psalms and Gospels* (Berkeley, 1963), pp. 3–11.

4. The subtitle of "The Church-porch" is "Perirrhanterium," or 'sprinkler.' Joseph H. Summers' beautiful critical study *George Herbert, His Religion and Art* (Cambridge, Mass., 1954) includes a brief discussion of typology (pp. 79–81). I am concerned here with the 'typical' structure of the entire *Temple;* Herbert's use of traditional types in individual poems is the subject of Rosemond Tuve's *A Reading of George Herbert* (Chicago, 1952). Fruitful discussions of the order in *The Temple* are R. L. Colie's "Logos in *The Temple," Journal of the Warburg and Courtauld Institute,* XXVI (1963), 327–342; Stanley Stewart's "Time and *The Temple,"Studies in English Literature,* VI (1966), 97–110; and John D. Walker's "The Architectonics of George Herbert's *The Temple,"* English Literary History, XXIX (1962), 289–305.

5. The three comings are distinguished, for example, in the collects for the Sundays of Advent in the Book of Common Prayer.

6. Milton's use of types has received scant attention. The only study devoted to the topic is William G. Madsen's recent *From Shadowy Types to Truth* (New Haven, 1968). Madsen deals extensively with seventeenth-century theories of biblical interpretation and discusses, at some length, the difference between his reading of Milton's symbolism and the views of previous critics. My intention, in this brief commentary on the first invocation, is only to make the reader aware of Milton's typological view of history, which enabled the poet to arrange all the details of *Paradise Lost* into one pattern. There is a good deal of incidental information on Milton's typology in John S. Coolidge's "Great Things and Small," *Comparative Literature,* XVII (1965), 1–23, and in Barbara K. Lewalski's "Structure and the Symbolism of Vision in Michael's Phrophecy, *PL* XI–XII," *Philological Quarterly,* XLII (1963), 25–35; see also Miss Lewalski's book on *Paradise Regained* entitled *Milton's Brief Epic* (Providence, 1966).

7. *Considerations Touching the Likeliest Means to Remove Hirelings out of the Church* (1659), Wm. B. Hunter, Jr., ed., *Prose,* Patrick, p. 487. On Milton's view of history, see Michael Fixler's *Milton and the Kingdoms of God* (Evanston, Ill., 1964).

8. *The Readie and Easie Way to Establish a Free Commonwealth* (1660), Barbara Kiefer Lewalski, ed., *Prose,* Patrick, p. 535.

9. Vaughan's originality is clearly demonstrated in the first part of Louis L. Martz's *The Paradise Within* (New Haven, 1964), pp. 3–31. Vaughan's use of typological images is still an unexplored topic. Again, my intention is to point to the presence of types in *Silex Scintillans,* in order to prevent the reader from assuming that Vaughan's imagery is private.

10. *The Nicene and Post-Nicene Fathers,* Philip Schaff, ed. (New York, 1886–1899; reprinted at Grand Rapids, Mich., 1956), first series, VII, 67.

11. *Ibid.,* first series, XII, 293.

12. Luther's gloss on Hebrews 11:19; *Luther: Early Theological Works,* trans. by James Atkinson, ed., *Library of Christian Classics,* XVI (Philadelphia, 1962), 219.

13. *Nicene . . . Fathers,* second series, V, 521.

# Suggestions for Further Reading

The scholar's pathway to seventeenth-century riches is the bibliography in Douglas Bush, *English Literature in the Earlier Seventeenth Century* (2nd edn., 1962), with which every student of the period ought to be on familiar terms. The suggestions given here supplement the references in the notes to the chapters and primarily draw attention to works that have appeared in the past six years.

Two articles define the achievement of modern scholarship; one is Sears Jayne's "Scholarship in the Renaissance," *Renaissance News* XVII (1964); the other is by Walter J. Ong, S. J., "Recent Studies in the English Renaissance," *Studies in English Literature*, IV (1964). The easiest means of keeping abreast of the volume of scholarly works on the seventeenth century is furnished by the reviews and abstracts in *Seventeenth-Century News,* a quarterly journal edited by J. Max Patrick and Harrison T. Meserole.

For original research on the social, economic, and political history of the period one would have to go to England to study the primary material available there. For an idea of the method of such research and of the variety of available manuscript sources the student should consult Lawrence Stone's *The Crisis of the Aristocracy, 1558–1641* (1965), especially the list on pp. xxi–xxiv. Many of the published primary sources are listed on pp. 401–402 of J. V. Akrigg's *Jacobean Pageant* (1962).

One of the foremost historians of the period is Christopher Hill; his *Society and Puritanism in Pre-Revolutionary England* may be supplemented by A. G. Dickens' *The English Reformation* (1964) and M. Walzer's *The Revolution of the Saints* (1965). An interesting survey is Maurice Ashley's *England in the Seventeenth Century* (1952), which differs in emphasis from Christopher Hill's *The Century of Revolution, 1603–1714* (1961). Ashley is also the author of a brilliant biography, *The Greatness of Oliver Cromwell* (1966). The royal actor in the Civil War is sympathetically rendered in C. V. Wedgwood's *A Coffin for King Charles* (1964). The major documents of the conflict have been reprinted in *The Puritan Revolution: A Documentary History,* S. E. Prall, ed. (1968). A similar collection dealing with Puritan opinions on Church issues is *The Reformation of the Church,* J. Murray, ed. (1964). The radical milennialists are the topic of P. G. Rogers' fascinating *The Fifth Monarchy Men* (1966).

The modern reader may be able to capture some of the flavor of life in the seventeenth century from *How They Lived, Vol. II: An Anthology of Original Accounts Written Between 1484 and 1700,* by M. Harrison and O. M. Royston (1964). Elizabeth Burton's *The Pageant of Stuart England* (1962) is a survey of manners, morals, foibles, and fashions. A more scholarly version of the same is the collection of Folger Library booklets *Life and Letters in Tudor and Stuart England,* L. B. Wright and, V. A. LaMar, eds. (1962).

One of the finest background studies, first published in French (1938), is now available in an English translation: Emile Bréhier's *The History of Philosophy: The*

*Seventeenth Century* (1966). A standard book on intellectual history is Ernst Cassirer's *The Individual and the Cosmos in Renaissance Philosophy* (1963). The rise of rationalism is treated by Henry G. Van Leeuven in *The Problem of Certainty in English Thought, 1630–1690* (1963). The struggle of reason versus faith is surveyed in D. C. Allen's encyclopedic *Doubt's Boundless Sea: Skepticism and Faith in the Renaissance* (1964). A reading of C. S. Lewis' *The Discarded Image* (1964) makes one aware of the debt that the seventeenth-century mind owes to medieval conceptions. Similarly 'conservative' is Robert Hoope's *Right Reason in the English Renaissance* (1962). *Jerusalem and Albion: The Hebraic Factor in Seventeenth-Century Literature* (1964), by Harold Fisch, demonstrates the influence of Protestant biblical interpretation. C. A. Patrides has written a book on the Christian view of history under the title *The Phoenix and the Ladder* (1964). The eschatology of the period is examined in D. P. Walker's *The Decline of Hell: Seventeenth-Century Discussions of Eternal Torment* (1964). The attitude towards science is treated in Nell Eurich's *Science in Utopia* (1967).

Some of the works that deal with the schooling of seventeenth-century minds have been referred to in notes 4, 8, 14, 21, 22, 25, 27, 29, and 35 to the first chapter. Additional information can be found in two recent important books: Kenneth Charlton's *Education in Renaissance England* (1965) and Joan Simon's *Education and Society in Tudor England* (1966). The rhetorical tradition in the schools of England is examined in a lucid article by Walter J. Ong, "Tudor Writings on Rhetoric," *Studies in the Renaissance,* XV (1968), which, among other things, presents Professor Ong's latest thoughts on the Ramist controversy. Frances A. Yates has examined a long neglected part of traditional rhetoric in *The Art of Memory* (1966). M. W. Croll was the first to demonstrate the importance of Renaissance rhetoric; his significant essays have been collected in *Style, Rhetoric, and Rhythm,* J. Max Patrick, R. O. Evans *et al.,* eds. (1966).

Cavalier poetry has received no mention in *The Temple of the Mind.* Its conventions are discussed in Chapter 2 of W. L. Chernaik's study of Waller, *The Poetry of Limitation* (1968). Especially commendable is A. W. Allison's *Toward an Augustan Poetic* (1962); Waller is the center of Allison's concern, but this brief study is also an admirable exposition of the development of the polite, social style in the verse of the age.

# Index